Studies in Amos

KYLE M. YATES, JR.

Convention Press

NASHVILLE   TENNESSEE

© 1966 • CONVENTION PRESS
Nashville, Tennessee

5102-31

TO MY PARENTS

WHOSE CHRISTIAN EXAMPLE

and

LOVE FOR THE BIBLE

laid the foundation for this volume

at an earlier date than they realized

Code Number: Church Study Course
This book is number 31 in category 2, section
for Adults and Young People

Library of Congress catalog card number: 66-22775
Printed in the United States of America
415. JUL 66 R.R.D.

About the Author

KYLE M. YATES, JR., was born January 11, 1924, in Louisville, Kentucky, where he received his public school education. His college work was begun at Mississippi College but interrupted by service in the Army Air Corps during World War II. After completing a tour of duty in Europe as a navigator, he finished his B.S. degree at Wake Forest College. Further study took him to the University of Edinburgh in Scotland and the University of Manchester in England. From Southern Baptist Theological Seminary he received the B.D. degree in 1951 and the Th.D. degree in 1955. He has done additional research and study at Harvard University.

He has served as pastor of churches in Kentucky and California. Since 1953 he has taught in the field of Old Testament and Archaeology at Golden Gate Baptist Theological Seminary, now located in Mill Valley, California.

He has written lessons for *Sunday School Married Young People*, teaching suggestions in *The Young People's Teacher*, and articles in various denominational periodicals. He has contributed other articles for *The Southern Baptist Encyclopedia*, *The Wycliffe Bible Commentary*, *The Wycliffe Bible Dictionary*, and *The Biblical World: A Dictionary of Biblical Archaeology*.

Dr. and Mrs. Yates have two children, a son David and a daughter Peggy.

Contents

Church Study Course

THE CHURCH STUDY COURSE began October 1, 1959. It is a merger of three courses previously promoted by the Sunday School Board —the Sunday School Training Course, the Graded Training Union Study Course, and the Church Music Training Course. On October 1, 1961, the Woman's Missionary Union principles and methods studies were added.

The course is fully graded. The system of awards provides a series of five diplomas of twenty books each for Adults or Young People, two diplomas of five books each for Intermediates, and two diplomas of five books each for Juniors.

The course is comprehensive, with books grouped into twenty categories. The purpose of the course is to help Christians to grow in knowledge and conviction, to help them to grow toward maturity in Christian character and competence for service, to encourage them to participate worthily as workers in their churches, and to develop leaders for all phases of church life and work.

The Church Study Course is promoted by the Baptist Sunday School Board, 127 Ninth Avenue, North, Nashville, Tennessee 37203, through its Sunday School, Training Union, Church Music, and Church Administration departments; by the Woman's Missionary Union, 600 North Twentieth Street, Birmingham, Alabama 35203; and by the respective departments in the states affiliated with the Southern Baptist Convention. A description of the course and the system of awards may be found in the leaflet "Trained Workmen," which may be obtained without charge from any one of these departments.

A record of all awards earned should be maintained in each church. A person should be designated by the church to keep the files. Forms for such records may be ordered from any Baptist Book Store.

Requirements for Credit in Class
or Home Study

IF CREDIT IS DESIRED for the study of this book in a class or by home study, the following requirements must be met:

I. IN CLASSWORK

1. The class must meet a minimum of seven and one-half clock hours. The required time does not include assembly periods. Ten class periods of forty-five minutes each are recommended. (If laboratory or clinical work is desired in specialized or technical courses, this requirement may be met by six clock hours of classwork and three clock hours of supervised laboratory or clinical work.)

2. A class member who attends all class sessions and completes the reading of the book within a week following the last class session will not be required to do any written work for credit.

3. A class member who is absent from one or more sessions must answer the questions (pp. 135–36) on all chapters he misses. In such a case, he must turn in his paper within a week, and he must certify that he has read the book.

4. The teacher should request an award for himself. A person who teaches a book in the section for Intermediates or Juniors (any category) or conducts an approved unit of instruction for Nursery, Beginner, or Primary children will be granted an award in category 11, Special Studies, which will count as an elective on his own diploma. He should specify in his request the name of the book taught, or the unit conducted for Nursery, Beginner, or Primary children.

5. The teacher should complete the "Request for Book Awards —Class Study" (Form 150) and forward it within two weeks after the completion of the class to the Church Study Course Awards Office, 127 Ninth Avenue, North, Nashville, Tennessee 37203.

II. In Home Study

1. A person who does not attend any class session may receive credit by answering all questions for written work as indicated in the book (pp. 135–36). When a person turns in his paper on home study, he must certify that he has read the book.

2. Students may find profit in studying the text together, but individual papers are required. Carbon copies or duplicates in any form cannot be accepted.

3. Home study work papers may be graded by the pastor or a person designated by him, or they may be sent to the Church Study Course Awards Office for grading. The form entitled "Request for Book Awards—Home Study" (Form 151) must be used in requesting awards. It should be mailed to Church Study Course Awards Office, 127 Ninth Avenue, North, Nashville, Tennessee 37203.

III. Credit for This Book

This book is number 31 in category 2 section for Adults and Young People.

CHAPTER 1

THE PROPHET AND HIS WORLD

1

The Prophet and His World

A STERN PROPHET dressed in rough clothes of animal skins, preaching fire and brimstone—this is often the mental picture called forth by the mention of Amos of Tekoa. Such a response is amazingly accurate but only partially true. For the picture should include more than an appearance which speaks of the past. There is the prophet's message to be considered. These words speak to the past, the present, and the future.

Amos was a person who could never be taken for granted. Whether one agreed with his views or not, the impact of the prophet's message was lasting. The past twenty-seven centuries have not blunted this impact. Any person who looks deeply into the character of this man of God, and studies seriously the message of the prophet, will never be the same. He cannot accept casually the injustices of present-day society nor overlook God's concern for all of his children.

I. THE MAN CALLED "PROPHET"

Many prophets during Israel's history could be recognized by appearance, emotional displays, or professional functions. Three Hebrew words are used to refer to the prophetic calling. Two of the words (*ro'eh* and *choseh*) are rendered "seer." The other (*navi*) is translated "prophet." The latter seems to give particular emphasis to the utterance or message. There were false prophets, cultic prophets, ecstatic prophets, and others related to the organized religious life of the community. However, Amos is not so easy to classify.

1

1. *His Status as a Layman* (7:14)

In answer to an opponent who tried to silence his preaching, Amos drew some clear lines of distinction about his ministry. He said, "I am no prophet, nor a prophet's son" (Amos 7:14, RSV). Thus he disavowed any contact with the prophetic guilds of his day or with those who practiced prophecy professionally. He claimed no degrees from accredited schools. He refused to claim Jerusalem or some local shrine as his base of operations or the source of his authority.

Having established his lay status in religious affairs, Amos described himself as a herdsman and a dresser of sycamore trees. His responsibility probably involved the caring for a special breed of small sheep, prized for the quality of their wool. The prophet furnished another interesting feature of his work by referring to his sideline as a cultivator of sycamore trees. These trees, quite different from the trees of the same name in America, were of the fig-mulberry classification. Attaining the size of a walnut tree, they provided much-needed shade in the hot and dry climate of Judah. More important for Amos was the fig-like fruit which grew in clusters on these trees. Amos' duties involved part-time cultivation of these trees, either artificially pollinating the trees or puncturing the ripening fruit.

The prophet's condemnation of luxury and his interest in the poor have caused many readers to think of him as belonging to the poorer class in society. However, Jewish tradition has long described him as a well-to-do sheep owner. This idea may be borne out by the word for "herdsman" used in Amos 1:1. In 2 Kings 3:4 it is translated "sheepmaster" or "sheep owner." Even if Amos owned his own sheep, the quality of pastureland available would suggest that his flock was not large.

2. *His Call* (7:15)

While engaged in his primary occupation of keeping his flock, Amos became conscious of a definite call from God.

His experience was quite removed from the center of organized religion at Jerusalem. During the course of humble duties, he had kept his mind open and attentive to the movement of God's spirit. As he faithfully watched over his sheep and their needs, he was awake to the word of God as it spoke of Israel's need.

Even though Amos was intent upon denying connection with the professional prophets, he was quick to acknowledge his relationship as God's prophet. God's command to him was specific: "Go, be a prophet to my people Israel." Amos wanted to make it perfectly clear that God was the source of his authority. He was responsible to none other, since he was commissioned to be God's spokesman. No institution or hierarchy could alter the purpose of the righteous God as it was unfolded to his servant. The prophet's attitude is reflected in these words: "The Lord God hath spoken, who can but prophesy?" (3:8).

3. His Character Traits

How can we evaluate the impact of a man removed many centuries from our day? It would be helpful to have an eyewitness report by one who heard Amos in the marketplace of Bethel. A record by one of the court historians would provide yet another viewpoint. No such report or record has been preserved to aid in an evaluation, but Amos projected his personality through his preaching and writing. With only the slightest reference to himself, his dominant nature shines through in every paragraph. Seven major traits become evident in a careful reading of his writing.

(1) *Simple.*—Amos came to town as a plain, homespun man without any pretense. His austere background as a nomad gave to him a note of genuineness which gained him a hearing. In the midst of a would-be sophisticated community, Amos appeared as a natural and unaffected voice out of the wilderness.

(2) *Stern.*—A large part of Amos' effectiveness came from his stern view of life and his blunt approach to its problems. No other prophet of Israel was so harsh and direct in dealing

with overt sin. He was hard, severe, and rigorous, whether speaking of sin or the sinner. To many who heard his messages, this trait may have been viewed as arrogance.

(3) *Keen.*—A simple, blunt person may obtain a hearing from a curious crowd; but he must have piercing insight to keep their attention. Surely few who heard Amos ever doubted that he was wide-awake, sharp, and discerning. His rough appearance contrasted with his high intelligence. His words were witness enough of his thoughtful and meditative depth.

(4) *Observant.*—Amos was no introspective mystic, concerned only with the small world around his flock of sheep. He demonstrated an astounding breadth of vision and insight. His knowledge of the world and its basic problems made possible penetrating observations. He was farsighted enough to be able to relate the history of his people to the scene of world history. Living in a remote region, he was nevertheless a citizen of the world.

(5) *Dynamic.*—Coupled with his bluntness was a certain dynamic appeal which came from his clear and incisive style of speaking and writing. His preaching may be characterized as worldwide in sweep, noble in imagery, and profound in intensity. His use of imagery demonstrated his keenness of mind as well as his close observation of nature and events. All of these factors added up to a style closely akin to the roar of a lion—a sound Amos knew so well.

(6) *Courageous.*—This prophet was no coward. He feared no man, prince or priest. His boldness and daring may have been a product of his self-reliance in the wilderness, but they were founded upon his deep confidence and trust in God.

(7) *Uncompromising.*—Above all, Amos was a man of principle who would not compromise his convictions nor water down the inflexible message of God. His rigid and strict approach to morals may have caused many of his hearers to regard him as prudish and puritanical. However, the depravity and injustice of Israel called for such a stand by the man of God.

II. The Setting of Amos' Ministry

Biblical truths can be applied best when the reader has a knowledge of the setting when God spoke. The teachings of God are timeless, but the application must be consistent with the original intent within the original setting. For this reason, Amos must be seen first as living and speaking to ancient Israel so that he may speak once again—this time to modern America.

1. *The Prophet's Relation to Judah*

Amos lived and labored in one of the most unpromising locations imaginable. His hometown was called Tekoa, a name probably referring to "the pitching of a tent." Prior to the division of the kingdom under Rehoboam, Tekoa was little more than a campsite. Its fame today is limited to its association with a lone prophet called of God from near its location.

The region around Tekoa is a vast wasteland, pitted with gullies which swiftly carry off water during the winter rains. Limestone hills with little vegetation dot the horizon to the north, south, and west. Even more desolate is the view to the east, where the land drops sharply toward the Dead Sea only eighteen miles away. This is the wilderness of Tekoa, remote and foreboding. Here Amos searched for pasture to sustain his flock. In this same area, down the slopes toward the Dead Sea, he cultivated his sycamore trees. In this desolate and silent world, Amos was made aware of the presence of God and realized his mission for God.

Yet, with all its detachment, Tekoa was only twelve miles from Jerusalem, the center of Judah's life. The Temple of Solomon had been standing for about two hundred years, making Jerusalem the hub of religious life for the Southern Kingdom of Judah. A deep heritage and many traditions had built up around this City of David. However, Amos never appealed to the example of Jerusalem, nor did he seek his authority there. He undoubtedly regarded himself as a citizen of Judah, but he remained aloof from the strong

urges of patriotism. He came out of the wilderness of Tekoa
with a loyalty toward God and the ideal which God had
laid upon his heart.

2. Amos' Mission to Israel

Why should Amos bypass Jerusalem with its many problems and go into the Northern Kingdom? Why should a
simple shepherd, living in the most detached area of Judah,
suddenly become concerned about foreign missions? Surely
the primary reason must be discerned in the pointed
mandate of God, "Go, prophesy unto my people Israel"
(7:15). Amos accepted this charge without question or pro-
test. Many experiences had prepared him for this high hour.
God did not break through into a vacuum but into a life
made well aware of the needs in Israel.

It is very likely that Amos had made previous journeys
to the markets in Israel. As a shepherd, he would have sold
his wool where the demand was greatest. Bethlehem lay
only six miles from Tekoa, Jerusalem twelve, and Bethel
twenty-two. Other places mentioned by Amos would have
been in easy reach; Samaria and Gilgal for instance. Tekoa
was within a walk of an hour and a half from an open view
of the land of the Philistines. The lands of Moab and Edom
were clearly visible from the wilderness of Tekoa.

It is surprising to find that Amos made mention of at least
thirty-eight cities and districts in the brief compass of his
writing. Through his travels, his contacts with traders and
merchants, and his keen observation of life, he was ready for
the task when God's call came to him. Amos' solitary life
had sharpened his eyes, intensified his ability to hear, and
quickened his conscience to respond.

In obedience to the summons of God, the prophet went to
Bethel, the site of the chief shrine for northern Israel. There
at a pilgrimage festival he preached his strong sermons
which finally brought him face to face with the priest
Amaziah (7:10–14). How many times he preached is a
moot question. It may be that he labored in Bethel, Gilgal,

and Samaria for brief periods. Then he might have gone back home to commit to writing the warnings which he had uttered and those messages which he had been prevented from preaching at Bethel.

3. Amos' Date in Historical Context

The scene for the ministry of Amos is tersely but systematically set in the opening verse of the book. No other prophetic book has so complete a superscription. Amos is mentioned, along with his primary occupation, his hometown, the area of his ministry, the kings of Judah and Israel. Even an event is mentioned as a means of orientation. The reference to Uzziah as king of Judah suggests approximate limits of 783 to 742 B.C. Corresponding almost exactly was the reign in Israel of Jeroboam II from 786 to 746 B.C.

Amos must have appeared on the scene during the latter part of Jeroboam's reign. The early years of Jeroboam's reign were spent in war to regain Israel's former status, whereas a time of peace and security pervaded the land in Amos' day. The evidence of prosperity and the wide-scale accumulation of wealth demand a date well into the reign of Jeroboam. Since Amos made no reference to the anarchy which followed the time of Jeroboam, it would seem that he completed his work before 746 B.C. It thus appears that the active ministry of Amos falls within the decade 760 to 750 B.C., though the length of his ministry cannot be fixed beyond question.

Amos is not mentioned elsewhere in the Scriptures, and many items about his life remain a complete mystery. We do not know when he was born, how old he was when he received God's call, how long he preached, how many years he lived, or how he died. Jewish tradition asserts that he met a martyr's death. One source suggests that he was killed by Uzziah, king of Judah. Another claims that he was murdered by Amaziah, the priest who opposed him at Bethel. The historical value of such traditions is certainly dubious.

III. The International Situation

In recent decades, Americans have become painfully aware of foreign affairs. The international situation often becomes the barometer of life and business. Such awareness has caused a new sense of the importance of political affairs relating to biblical times, even those involving nations other than the people of God. Since ancient Israel was so often oppressed, and even more often threatened by outsiders, the international scene becomes a dominant issue. Especially is this point true for the book of Amos. The prophet of Tekoa was extremely conscious of the threatening doom coming as the judgment of God but administered by a foreign army. He was likewise acquainted with affairs of historical import which were completely overlooked by the majority of Israel's populace.

1. *The Balance of Power*

The fortunes of ancient Israel were subject to rise and fall in proportion to the relative strength of the rival powers on the international scene. By the time of Amos, great empires had already waxed and waned. The major balance of power had long been established between Egypt and the Mesopotamian kingdoms. There were further checks and balances between lesser powers, which brought about times of peace and prosperity.

In 805 B.C. an event occurred which turned the fortunes of Israel. The Assyrians crushed Damascus (Syria) and thus allowed Jehoash to recapture much of the territory lost by his father Jehu. Into such a promising situation came Jeroboam II, who enjoyed even greater military success than his predecessors. He was able to restore all the territory previously lost by Israel and add to his kingdom in every direction, even capturing Damascus itself. Thus he effectively controlled almost all the area once held by David, except for the smaller kingdom of Judah. As Amos came on the scene, during the latter half of Jeroboam's reign, a balance in power had produced a time of relative peace. Assyria had effectively reduced the strength of Syria. Then Assyria entered a period of decline due to a series of weak kings. Since Egypt was likewise weak, there was no dominant power on the international scene. The absence of one overpowering nation made possible for Israel the greatest era of peace which she had known as an independent kingdom.

2. *The Lull Before the Storm*

Even in the midst of peace and prosperity, the dark clouds of war were threatening on the horizon. The rising power of the Assyrians seems to have been ignored by leaders and people alike. But not by Amos! To him, judgment seemed inevitable. He felt it would come in the form of devastation by war. Defeat and exile would complete the cycle of events. Although Assyria is not specifically named, Amos used veiled references which clearly implied that God would use the Assyrian power to accomplish his purposes.

About the time of Jeroboam's death, a new king, Tiglath-pileser III, took over in Assyria and quickly established himself as a threat to Syria and Israel. Within a few years he had conquered Syria and taken captives from Galilee. It was only about twenty-five years after the death of Jeroboam that Samaria fell and Israel went into captivity. The doom, which Amos so clearly saw and so fearlessly proclaimed, had arrived!

IV. LIFE IN ISRAEL AND JUDAH

In order to make the book of Amos live, we must be able to identify with the people involved. The individuals originally addressed by the messenger of God must come alive. We must see them as real persons. We need to sense how the wealthy secular-minded person responded to Amos' message and justified his way of life. We need to be sensitive to the deeper feelings of the poor and mistreated. We need to perceive the attitude of the average "man on the street" who may or may not fall into either classification. We must also keep in mind that there were God-fearing men and women who recognized the evils about them but merely kept silent. Although they were not singled out by Amos, his message was applicable to them.

1. *Economic Background*

Amos came upon the scene at Bethel well aware of the booming economy of the Northern Kingdom under Jeroboam II. Peace had made possible once again the control of the great trade routes which ran north and south through the country. A strong merchant class had arisen during the hectic days just past. The small businessmen had been forced out. Their properties had been grabbed by those building great estates. The newly rich merchants and landowners had found a place at the top of the social ladder. There was still no real middle class. The rich were busy building and enjoying their winter houses and their summer houses—terminology used by Amos but probably rarely heard before his day.

The average man lived a simple type of life. While he was either a farmer or a shepherd, he usually lived in a small town or village for protection from enemy attack. Several towns were further guarded by connection with a strongly fortified city nearby. Amos fully realized the difficulties during a time of siege (as he pointed out in chapter 6 of his book). There was usually no systematic planning in the villages or the cities. Most of the houses were crudely built, ranging from one-room huts to more stable houses arranged around an open courtyard. Some of the latter consisted of two stories, the lower used for household chores and storage, the second floor for sleeping. The roofs, normally of straw mixed with mud and lime, had to be repaired after every strong rain. Furniture seldom was found except in the homes of the wealthy.

The diet of the average Israelite further indicates the simplicity of his life. Bread was the basic item. Usually it was made into flat cakes from barley or wheat mixed with olive oil. Vegetables included horsebeans, lentils, and cucumbers. Some variety of the menu of the bread and vegetables was possible by the addition of onions, garlic, or leeks as flavoring. Grapes, figs, dates, pomegranates, syca- more figs, and raisins played an important part in the diet. Meat was normally reserved only for special occasions such as festivals and feasts.

The division of the rich and poor could also be seen in the typical clothing. Garments of the well-to-do class were carefully dyed with costly purple and elaborately decorated with fringes and tassels along the borders of the cloth. The poorer person wore a simple tunic covered by a cloak of wool, linen, or skins. The women and the elders wore long tunics. A workman or warrior probably wore a short tunic with a "T-shirt" type of covering for his upper body.

2. Social Problems

To the outsider, Israel's economic outlook might have appeared encouraging. But it did not seem so to the prophet from Tekoa. He could sense the mutter of discontent on every side. Even more, he could see the moral decay be- neath the veneered surface.

(1) *Luxury and extravagance.*—Luxury among the wealthy was apparent. Many Israelites interpreted this as an evident token of God's blessings of peace and prosperity on their land. The houses of hewn stone, the ivory-paneled walls, the furniture of inlaid ivory, and the cushions of silk were not evil in themselves. The evil which Amos recog- nized was in the contrast of luxury with the conditions of people in the lower class. Society was organized in such a way that equality of opportunity was impossible. The "have's" had no concern about the necessities of the "have- not's." The primary thought among the wealthy was how they might increase their own possessions.

(2) *Injustice and dishonesty.*—Amos saw in the un- bridled luxury a deeper problem than the inequalities be- tween the two classes. The wealthy had gained their posi- tion not by honest toil but by oppression and injustice. For a trifling debt, a poor man was sold into slavery or his

children were taken from him. Justice was sold to the one who could pay the highest bribe or offer the costliest present. The widow, orphan, or alien had little chance for justice. The merchants had their special weights and measures always ready for the unsuspecting buyer or the one whose complaint would not be taken seriously. The small holdings of land were being steadily taken from the poor by unscrupulous men intent upon building great estates.

(3) *Immorality and self-indulgence.*—Amos abhorred the excesses of the nation's leaders. The perpetual feasting and revelry of the wealthy presented a sharp contrast to the suffering of the masses. Some even used bowls for their wine, and the society women were able to keep up with the men in their drinking. Although the prophet only once mentioned sexual immorality, he left an indelible picture of debauchery (2:7–8).

3. Religious Factors

The deplorable social problems were compounded by a mixed-up religious system. The Mosaic faith had been watered down by the addition of pagan practices and symbols. Some of these pagan factors had been introduced by the Canaanites who remained in the land after the conquest. Golden images of young bulls had been set up at Bethel and Dan by Jeroboam I, when the kingdoms divided at the time of Solomon's death. Other pagan practices crept in through Jezebel and the tolerant attitude of Ahab.

In order to understand Amos' great concern, it is imperative that we recognize the insidious nature of the Canaanite or Tyrian Baal worship. Baal worship was inseparably linked with the cycles of nature throughout the year. The earth was viewed as dead during the dry summer months and could be revived only by awaking the deities of fertility. This was believed to be accomplished by the physical union of men and women in acts of prostitution in the name of religion. Thus by sympathetic magic, fertility was supposed to come to all of life—field, flock, husband and wife alike.

Not only were the lowest aspects of human desire brought

into the faith of Israel, but the basic essentials of Mosaic faith were treated in a hopelessly superficial manner. "Church" attendance was good; sacrifices and offerings were abundant; tithes were multiplied. Yet, to the prophet these things appeared as mere ritual, going through the motions in the name of religion. There was no deeply spiritual effect upon the conduct of the people when they left the shrine.

Such was the moral and spiritual level of the Israel to which Amos addressed himself. Is it any wonder that he thundered as a young lion?

FOR CLASS PREPARATION

1. Compare the call of Amos (7:14ff.) with that of Isaiah (Isa. 6:1ff.).
2. Draw up a list in two columns of the plus and minus factors in the personality makeup of Amos.
3. Consider seriously and write a paragraph on your opinion of the effect of Amos' life in the wilderness of Tekoa upon his readiness to respond to God's call.
4. Make a list of parallels between Israel in Amos' day and contemporary America in regard to economic, social, and religious problems.

For Advanced Study [1]

1. For a summary of statements evaluating the impact of Amos:
   A. C. Knudson, *The Beacon Lights of Prophecy*, p. 57–58.
   R. L. Honeycutt, *Amos and His Message*, p. 2.
   K. M. Yates, Sr., *Preaching from the Prophets*, pp. 40–41.
2. For a description of the rugged country around Tekoa:
   G. A. Smith, *The Book of the Twelve Prophets*, I, pp. 72ff.
3. For a vivid picture of the daily life of the Israelites:
   G. E. Wright, *Biblical Archaeology* (rev. ed., 1962) pp. 183ff.
   M. S. and J. L. Miller, *Encyclopedia of Bible Life*.
   E. W. Heaton, *Everyday Life in Old Testament Times*.
4. For a more comprehensive view of Baal worship:
   G. E. Wright, *Biblical Archaeology*, pp. 107–120.
   W. F. Albright, *Archaeology and the Religion of Israel*, pp. 68–94.

---

[1] These suggestions have been included by the author for those who wish to engage in greater depth study of the book of Amos. (Some books are now out of print but may be available in a library.) Inclusion of these books does not indicate endorsement of total content by either the author or publisher of STUDIES IN AMOS.

CHAPTER 2

THE PROPHET AND HIS MESSAGE

2

The Prophet and His Message

FOR MANY PEOPLE the mainspring of all prophecy is prediction. A true prophet, according to such a concept, is one who
can foretell future events. Therefore, many interpreters of
the Bible have sought for fulfilment of words never meant
to be applied literally to the future. There are those today
who read the writings of the prophets with an eye only to
the signs of our time, in order to link up contemporary
events and persons.

While there are elements of prediction in the preaching
of Amos, he was speaking primarily to the people of his day.
Although many things came to pass as promised, we must
not make literal fulfilment of his various messages the test of
their value. God inspired Amos to read the signs of his own
time. He gave him remarkable insight into political events
and their providential significance. This is not to say that
the message of Amos cannot be applied to another age.
However, the first and foremost responsibility of Amos was
to speak as a witness to the needs of God's people in the
eighth century B.C.

I. THE CONTRIBUTIONS OF FORMER PROPHETS

The prophets were not isolated individuals, divorced from
dependence upon one another. The four great prophets of
the eighth century B.C.—Amos, Hosea, Isaiah, and Micah—
had in common an underlying unity of spirit and purpose,
although they differed greatly in personality and presentation of their respective messages. Each of them owed a debt
to those who had prepared the way for his ministry as a
spokesman for God.

16

1. *The Heritage of Past Spokesmen*

Amos was probably the earliest prophet to have his messages preserved in a book bearing his name. However, there was already a long history of prophetic activity. Much that had gone under the name of prophecy had been inferior to the dynamic preaching of Amos. There were many seers whose main emphasis had been soothsaying, divination, or clairvoyance. There were those who, calling themselves prophets, escaped reality by means of trances and ecstatic states. There were others who always adjusted their messages to the pleasure of the one or ones who paid their salaries. Then there were true spokesmen who were worthy predecessors to Amos and the other writing prophets.

Moses stands at the head of the list, although we usually think of him as a lawgiver, a mediator, or a special type of leader. (See Hos. 12:13*a;* Deut. 34:10, RSV.) Moses performed the function of a prophet and left his mark upon the soul of Israel.

Samuel is remembered as a judge, a priest, a man of prayer, and a prophet. It was in the latter capacity that he excelled, becoming God's spokesman in a dark time of Israel's history. His work with the young prophets was significant for its relationship to a movement quite extreme in ecstatic behavior.

Elijah must also be considered in the context of Amos' ministry. His example on Mount Carmel set the stage for Amos at Bethel. Elijah's concern for social justice in the vineyard of Naboth made him a "blood brother" of Amos. To no other prophet was Amos so indebted for the substance of his messages on the oppression of the poor in Israel. Elisha is associated with the name of Elijah. Although he carried the mantle of Elijah, his temperament did not make him an exact link between Elijah and Amos.

Two lesser known prophets contributed to Amos' heritage as a spokesman for God. Nathan's pointed rebuke of David, "Thou art the man" (2 Sam. 12:7), demonstrated his stature as a worthy predecessor of Amos. Micaiah proved himself within the same tradition as he faced Ahab and Jehoshaphat with God's message of judgment (1 Kings 22:15–28). These two men, barely remembered in the general history of God's people, represent others who spoke for God and should take their places in the heritage of prophetic witnesses.

2. *The Prophetic Guilds*

In Israel there was an established order of prophets, corresponding in some ways to the priesthood but differing in function. While the priests concentrated upon the law and the sacrificial system, the prophets were more interested in God's word or answer for society.

In 1 Samuel 10:5–13, Saul was instructed by Samuel to join himself to a band of prophets moving about the country. They carried a variety of musical instruments and apparently engaged in rather frenzied activity. Extreme in their zeal, these early bands of prophets had an intense loyalty to both God and country.

Less than two centuries later, large groups of official prophets were again mentioned. Elijah described how he saved one hundred of the Lord's prophets when Jezebel was on one of her prophet-killing sprees (1 Kings 18:13). Four hundred and fifty prophets of Baal and four hundred prophets of Asherah were mentioned in the story of Elijah's challenge on Mount Carmel (1 Kings 18:19). Four hundred prophets were consulted as a group prior to Micaiah's appearance before Ahab and Jehoshaphat (1 Kings 22:6). Such groups were brotherhoods, or guilds, living in a semi-monastic fashion. While some may have supported themselves, the majority were probably dependent upon those whom they served.

The fact that Amos disassociated himself from any professional order of prophets may indicate that he repudiated their excessive ecstasy, their commercialism, or that he was asserting his own independence. Whatever his motive, Amos accepted the best within his heritage and blazed a trail for other prophets to follow. His independence was in reality an utter dependence upon God, which gave a new sense of inspiration to his message.

II. The Burden of Amos' Preaching

The call experienced by Amos definitely determined his function as that of a prophet, his authority as being from God, and his field of service as Israel. The character of his message must be surmised from the book itself. It is obvious that his message was a burden to be borne directly to the people. So far as we know, Amos never sought audience with the king or the leaders. He poured out his words in impassioned appeal to the crowds gathered in Israel. There was something compulsive about the way he preached—a compulsion born of God's Spirit. God had clearly spoken; what could Amos do but prophesy?

1. *The Dominant Themes*

Can the teaching of the book of Amos be condensed into a few ideas? If this is accomplished, will we be able to see one main theme shining through? Many writers have assumed that both are possible. Yet, the search for a dominant theme has taken scholars in several directions.

It is possible to find the key to the preaching of Amos in the words: "Let justice roll down like waters, and righteousness like an everflowing stream" (5:24, RSV). Certainly this union of justice and righteousness in daily life was a burden upon his heart. Every contact with the people, every business dealing with the merchants, and every observation of the superficial religious activities deepened this burden. On the other hand, a large share of the prophet's attention was directed toward the certainty of doom about to befall the nation. Amos was never able to get far away from the reality of the judgment of God. He kept coming back to this theme, filling his messages with concrete illustrations and vivid descriptions.

These two themes seem inseparably bound up in the proclamation of God's purpose through Amos: Because God is righteous and just, he demands a corresponding justice and righteousness from his people. Yet, since injustice and oppression had triumphed in Israel, the corollary of justice, which is judgment, was inevitable. In keeping with this theme, Amos continued a two-pronged attack. Constantly he wove together a call for justice while announcing the certain doom.

A major question concerns what Amos really hoped to accomplish. Many scholars have thought of him as a prophet of doom, one who expressed no hope. The concluding section of his book (9:11-15) has often been treated as a reversal of his entire message. While the transition from doom to hope is rather abrupt, a conclusion based on hope is essential in light of the certainty of punishment. Amos showed no expectation of national repentance as a consequence of his preaching, since the people were too deeply involved in sin and the luxuries of their boom economy. All Amos could hope to accomplish was that some of his hearers would experience quickening of conscience and preparation of mind for the coming exile. Looking beyond the immediate future, Amos saw the only answer to Israel's problem in the hands of a small remnant.

Such a sense of hope was essential to the completion of Amos' call for justice and his enunciation of doom. Beyond the exile there had to be a new day in which God's purpose for Israel would be realized. If a remnant was to be kept alive toward that day, a new sense of righteousness and justice had to be deeply ingrained into the hearts and minds of those about to enter the exile. Only a prophet of righteousness, such as Amos, could lay this foundation for the new era.

2. The Related Subjects

Although Amos was very consistent in charting a course and staying with it, several other aspects of his teaching become apparent. Because of his keen observation of problems within Israel and abroad, Amos presented many facets of man's relation with God. These deserve special note.

(1) *The sovereignty of God.*—Amos saw God as personally in control of all the world. Amos made clear that, contrary to the view within pagan religions and among the
majority of Israelites, God was not only the God of Israel
but of all the world. While the average Israelite may have
remembered with national pride the special place of Israel's
exodus from Egypt, Amos maintained that God was also
behind the early movements of the Philistines and Ara-
maeans (9:7).

Just as God is the Lord of history, he is also the Lord
of nature. The tie between these two realities is important
for understanding Amos' thought. He saw God's sovereignty
through nature *over* man. Amos proclaimed God as controlling all the forces of nature from earth to heaven and even
to the bottom of the sea. As creator and sustainer God uses
plague, eclipse, or other phenomena to bless or to punish.

Amos viewed God as dealing out punishment according
to his standard of righteousness. The nations were to be
punished impartially in relation to God's ethical standards.
They were promised judgment for their offences against
moral decency, not just for sins against the people of God.
On this basis God demanded righteous behavior, just as he
ruled in righteousness and judged by righteous criteria. This
concept of God was the foundation upon which all other
teachings in Amos were built.

(2) *The relationship between privilege and responsibility.*—For Amos, the greatness of God presented a challenge
to righteous living and a duty involving heavier responsibility on Israel's part. As a specially chosen people, Israel must
be doubly accountable to God. The leaders of Israel tended
to recognize the greatness of God primarily as a national
asset, imparting greatness and prestige to the nation. These
leaders, and the mass of the people who followed blindly,
were dazzled by the military and economic success of Jeroboam's reign. They viewed their unparalleled prosperity as
a sign of God's favor, thinking that their place of privilege
was an insurance that all was well.

With a note of austerity, Amos dispelled the thinking that

the people were safe in their affluent society. He called them back to the basic principle of life: Being chosen of God means immeasurably more responsibility, not distinctive privilege or special exemptions.

(3) *The curse of unconcern.*—Amos was constantly upset by the lack of concern on the part of God's people. In the marketplace he observed the indifference to the cries of the poor. In the palaces he could see no thought given for the oppressed. Even at the sanctuaries, the deepest needs of the downtrodden were completely ignored.

Amos directed his denunciations of the idle rich and the crooked merchants mainly toward their unconcern and injustice. While he was aware of their unethical methods, his most devastating condemnation was aimed at their callous disregard of the rights and necessities of others. In their ease, luxury, and idleness the rich were unwilling to consider the suffering and distress of the less fortunate.

(4) *The basis of true religion.*—No one can read the book of Amos and miss seeing how disgusting the religious practices of Israel appeared to the prophet. The problem was not one of awakening zeal, since everywhere he saw the observance of rites and ceremonies. The externals of religious observances were evident at shrines and sanctuaries. Yet, Amos recognized that the sacrifices and offerings were meaningless. In fact, he classed them as insults to God, since they were divorced from any relationship to moral obligations. The worshiper appeared to believe that God would overlook his moral delinquencies as long as he offered sufficient sacrifices and made frequent religious pilgrimages.

The purpose of Amos in decrying the prevailing practices in religious expression was not to destroy all corporate worship. Rather, he sought to link worship with the daily life of the average man. He longed for the type of dealings in business and family which would demonstrate a heartfelt experience with God. He was seeking to set forth the vital connection between the worship of a righteous God and righteousness in the life of a people.

III. The Content of the Book

The book of Amos quite clearly bears the marks of the age in which it was written. The keen awareness of current events, the vivid descriptions of social ills, and the precise analysis of empty religion present a striking picture of life in a momentous period of Israel's history. This picture is carefully woven into a definite plan with logical development and superb literary skill.

1. Style

That Amos was a literary artist is generally accepted, but why this should be so is difficult to understand. His background in the wilderness of Tekoa would hardly suggest that Amos should rank among the greatest of Old Testament prophets in literary merit. Yet, it seems evident that command of language and ready pen were a part of the training of Amos for God's call.

The book of Amos moves forward in a forceful and dramatic way. Never is there uncertainty as to the final result. The language is usually clear and pure. The sentences are carefully constructed and flow evenly, paragraph after paragraph. There is also a rhythmic quality which ranks Amos' use of poetry among the best within the prophetic literature. The poetic effect is further strengthened by effective contrasts and refrains, telling repetitions, play on words, irony and sarcasm.

His striking use of imagery puts Amos in a class by himself. His figures of speech are always used with refreshing naturalness. Never do they detract from the message nor break the sequence of thought. The young lion roaring over his prey (3:4), the net springing up to trap the bird (3:5), the shepherd recovering the remnant of a sheep out of the lion's mouth (3:12), and the locust devouring vegetation (7:1–2) are all graphic symbols of life in progress. Yet, they are far more than interesting sidelights, since they are interpreted and applied by the insight of a prophet who could translate his astute observations into well-chosen words.

2. Organization

The book of Amos is well organized and moves gradually toward the completion of its theme. The progress of thought breaks naturally into three sections, plus an epilogue.

(1) *The preamble* (1:1 to 2:16).—After the terse title which sets the stage, the first section opens with a roar of denunciation. In rapid succession the best known neighbors of Israel are paraded into view. Amos uses a dramatic series of oracles of the same form to condemn the most flagrant crimes of each nation. The condemnations reach a climax in the more detailed denunciation of the gross injustices within Israel. Coupled with the accounts of injustice is the warning of doom which completes the dominant theme within the first cycle of addresses.

(2) *The charges* (3:1 to 6:14).—The second section consists of a series of messages which spell out in more detail the charges against Israel. The introductory words, "Hear this word," occur three times (3:1; 4:1; 5:1) and, thereby, herald a new series of charges. The solemn warning, "Woe," may further divide the last message (5:18; 6:1). It should be noted that Amos begins this section with a warning of judgment and constantly reminds his hearers of its certainty (3:15; 4:3; 4:12; 5:17, 27; 6:14). Instead of building up to the prospect of judgment, he begins and ends with it, weaving in the charges against Israel which made the judgment necessary. The series of messages closes with the verdict of a coming captivity administered by a nation raised up for the purpose.

(3) *The visions* (7:1 to 9:10).—The third section differs from the previous messages in form but not in basic content or purpose. There are five visions which emphasize the certainty of the approaching doom. The first two are drawn from the realm of nature, picturing disasters as illustrative of Israel's punishment. The third comes from history, portraying God in the process of checking Israel against a plumb line. The fourth is drawn from a scene in the market, representing Israel at the end of the way as a basket of ripe

summer fruit. The fifth centers upon a scene at a religious sanctuary, depicting the hopelessness of escape from God's punishment. Added to the visions are explanatory comments, added by the prophet to make sure the meaning is grasped.

The historical episode, describing Amos' encounter with Amaziah at Bethel (7:10–17), breaks the sequence of visions but gives an indispensable picture of Amos in action. The section closes with a ray of hope that the captivity may prove to be discipline rather than utter doom.

(4) *The epilogue* (9:11–15).—The theme of social injustice bringing doom passes swiftly to hope for a new day. Out of the turmoil and destruction of battle and captivity will come a brighter future. While such a hope seems strange in light of the finality of judgment preached by Amos, it is thoroughly in keeping with the justice and purpose of God as seen by Amos. Such a restoration is the only logical conclusion which can complete the process of righteous punishment upon God's people.

IV. THE RELEVANCE OF THE MESSAGE

While a study of the book of Amos from a historical standpoint is rewarding and intriguing, our greatest concern is, How does Amos speak to our day and to the problems facing us? It should be apparent already that Amos addressed himself to problems which are very much a part of our society. The answers he gave are based upon an intimate knowledge of God and his purposes. These answers are not theoretical solutions; they are practical conclusions, well illustrated with experience from life and fellowship with God. Although there are extreme differences between the simple life of eighth century B.C. and the technological life of the twentieth century A.D., the basic problems and the fundamental principles remain much the same. Sin is still sin, and injustice is injustice. The book of Amos may not speak *of* our age, but it certainly speaks *to* our age in a loud, clear voice.

Recurring thoughout the book are three points which are

most relevant for our consideration: *divine sovereignty, social justice,* and *true worship.* Other topics will be found applicable, but these three should be kept foremost throughout the study of the book of Amos. These three themes remain dominant in this prophetic book.

1. Emphasis upon Divine Sovereignty

While the majority of Americans today express some degree of belief in God, the dominant pattern of life is "practical atheism." By this term we mean that in some semi-religious way the existence of God may be admitted, but the sovereignty of God is ignored. For all practical purposes, multitudes have rejected God's right to enter into the affairs of men.

Again and again Amos will call us back to the realization of God's control and rule over all of creation. We will become increasingly aware of God's concern for all persons. We will be reminded of our place of privilege within the plan of God. However, Amos will not let us rest upon our privileged status. He will prod us into accepting the responsibilities involved. His blunt but forceful speech will leave no doubt as to the futility of trying to escape from the presence of God. His pronouncement of utter destruction upon Israel as righteous retribution will make us wonder how long God's patience can last in our day.

2. Clarion Call for Social Justice

Many persons today see little relationship between religion and ethical responsibility. Many place great emphasis upon correct belief and formal religious duties. Yet, they do not connect these with what Jesus called "the weightier matters of the law" (Matt. 23:23). Others reverse the emphasis, forgetting that duty to society is inseparably linked with their relationship to a just God.

While we observe Amos denouncing specific social ills of his day, we shall see him repeatedly pointing an accusing finger at sore spots in our own society. As a result, we may become less impressed by advances made in civilization at the cost of concern for the oppressed, the hungry, and the forgotten of the world. We may no longer be able to look the other way when we see dishonesty, bribery, cruelty, injustice, and intolerance in our land. It may be that we will become just as sensitive to the inhumanities within our nation as we now are to those of the Nazis or the Communists. The burning words of Amos will make us aware that the righteous God is concerned about every phase of life. He demands a standard of righteousness which staggers the imagination, even of a twentieth-century Christian.

3. *Insight into the Basis of True Worship*

A variety of activities are called "worship" by religious groups in our day. The current attitude in many circles is that it does not really matter what one believes nor how one worships, so long as he is sincere in it.

Amos' words on "worship" may shock us. He spoke of much of it as being an insult to God, not because of the form or the content of the worship but because of the follow-up. His words may cause us to ask ourselves some serious questions about the ends which we seek in worship. We may find that our experience with God is not real enough to reach out into the rest of the week. Above all, we may discover that neither the elaborate nor the simple ceremony of worship can be used as a substitute for moral justice and righteousness in daily life. There is probably no more relevant truth in the book of Amos for our society than this principle.

A. F. Kirkpatrick has adequately summed up these aspects of the central issues in Amos, saying:

The Book of Amos teaches, with singular clearness and force, truths which can never become superfluous or obsolete. The truths that justice between man and man is one of the divine foundations of society; that privilege implies responsibility, and that failure to recognise responsibility will surely bring punishment; that nations, and by analogy, individuals, are bound to live up to that measure of light and knowledge which has been granted to them; that the most elaborate worship is but an insult to God when offered by those who have no mind to

conform their wills and conduct to His requirements;—these
are elementary but eternal truths.[1]

FOR CLASS PREPARATION

1. Compare the work of a professional prophet in 1 Samuel 9:
   6–10 and Micah 3:5–11 with the life of a member of a prophetic guild in 1 Samuel 10:5–13; 1 Kings 22:6; and 2 Kings
   2:3–5. Now contrast the impact of these prophets with what
   you know about Amos.
2. Make a list of passages in Amos announcing and describing
   doom upon Israel. Study them in the light of the dominant
   theme suggested in the discussion of this chapter.
3. Check the areas of relevance mentioned in the chapter against
   your needs and those of your church, community, and nation.
   Try to imagine what Amos might say to those needs.

FOR ADVANCED STUDY

1. For a review of prophetic activity before the time of Amos:
   G. A. Smith, *The Book of the Twelve Prophets,* pp. 10–40.
   A. C. Knudson, *The Prophetic Movement in Israel,* pp. 11–40.
   R. S. Cripps, *The Book of Amos,* pp. 14–22.
2. For a summary of the problems surrounding the unity of authorship:
   R. L. Honeycutt, *Amos and His Message, pp.* 15–17.
   S. R. Driver, *Joel and Amos* (Cambridge Bible), pp. 117–124.
   H.E.W. Fosbroke, "The Book of Amos," *The Interpreter's Bible* VI,
   pp. 722–775.
3. For a discussion of the prophetic view of God:
   J. P. Hyatt, *Prophetic Religion,* pp. 149–161.
4. For a broad view of the perennial value of the prophets:
   R.B.Y. Scott, *The Relevance of the Prophets,* pp. 204–207.

---

[1] A. F. Kirkpatrick, *The Doctrine of the Prophets* (3rd ed.; New York:
The Macmillan Company, 1912), p. 104.

CHAPTER 3

A CATALOG OF ATROCITIES—AMOS 1–2

3

A Catalog of Atrocities

AMOS 1–2

IN MOST CIVILIZATIONS it is relatively easy to collect a crowd. There have always been the Hyde Parks, the Central Parks, and the Boston Commons, where individuals could mount their soapboxes. In ancient days, the city gate and the marketplace were the natural gathering places where one's voice could be heard. Because of the innate curiosity of mankind, a commanding figure can draw a group of people around him. However, keeping the attention of such a crowd is difficult. Amos not only commanded a hearing by the uniqueness of his appearance; he kept his audience by superb presentation.

I. THE APPROACH OF AMOS

The opening sermon in the book of Amos presents the prophet of Tekoa at his best. He stands as a master orator, the prophetic example for future prophets of Israel. While there is no question but that he was speaking a genuine message of God, the approach was his own. Like all true prophets, he was inspired in a very real way. Yet, his personality shone through his message. The Spirit of God moved in and through the human vessel. The Lord was not speaking in a "still small voice" to an Elijah but was roaring as a lion through the austere prophet from Tekoa (1:2).

1. Applied Psychology

It was probably on a festive occasion, a religious or civic festival, when Amos stood up to speak. The crowds had assembled from many parts of Israel. They had not come to hear a sermon, nor were they in any mood for the cutting message they were about to hear. Rather than open with a broadside denunciation, Amos showed great wisdom in adapting his method of presentation to the occasion. He caught and held their attention until his climax was reached.

In rapid succession, Amos lashed out against six of Israel's traditional enemies, pointing out their sins and the certainty of their punishment. Appealing to the patriotism and nationalism of his hearers, the prophet was able to gain their sympathetic attention. From this point of common agreement, he led his audience slowly toward his main premise. With each reference to a neighboring nation, he was able to involve the people more deeply. Each amen, nod of a head, and shout of approval further identified the hearers with the herdsman–prophet from the wilderness. Each point of agreement made it more difficult to reject, without serious thought, his indictments upon Judah and Israel. The air of excitement surrounding the series of denunciations made all the more striking the solemn silence and then angry outcry when Israel was condemned.

However, the psychological buildup to the promise of judgment upon Israel was no oratorical trick to win a sympathetic hearing. There was a theological purpose behind Amos' approach. The prophet was building up to a dramatic and intentional climax. Once the people had agreed, silently or vocally, that judgment must come upon the other nations, the ground was prepared for Israel's recognition of her own doom. If God would judge those who did not know his law, how much more would he bring punishment upon those who had received but rejected his teachings?

Lest any within Israel should claim immunity because of special status, Amos clearly pointed to a difference in the type of sin without and within Israel. George Adam Smith sharply distinguished these as sins of barbarism for Israel's neighbors and sins of civilization within Israel. Whereas the sins of the outsiders were related to treaties and war, the sins of God's people were domestic injustices with strong moral principles involved. In building up from isolated acts

of barbarism outside to the continued life of injustice within
Israel, Amos was pointing to the subtle cruelty involved in
injustice and oppression. The sins of civilization may not
reach the headlines as often as the atrocities of barbarism,
but they eat away at the very soul of a nation.

2. *Purposeful Plan*

Amos' careful plan of the oracles against the nations is
quickly recognized by the reader. However, determining
his premeditated plan is quite difficult.

It has often been suggested that a geographical framework is dominant. The scene opens in the northeast (Damascus), moves to the southwest (Philistia), jumps to the
northwest (Phoenicia), and passes to the southeast (Edom,
Ammon, Moab). Amos may have had in mind a cosmic significance connected with "the four corners of the earth." He
may also have envisioned a huge circle with enemy nations
on the circumference and the people of God in the center.

A historical framework is also possible. The prophet may
have begun with Damascus because she was the major rival
of Israel, and then moved on to Philistia as Damascus' ally
in an attack upon Israel (Isa. 9:12). Tyre may have been
mentioned next because of the similarity of indictment with
that of Philistia. Edom would logically follow since she was
the recipient of the ill-gotten slaves from Tyre. Ammon and
Moab were likewise historically connected with the affairs
of Edom.

An ethical framework is certainly possible. A close analysis
of the crimes shows three basic categories: (1) cruelty in war
(Damascus, Ammon); (2) enslaving captives (Philistia,
Phoenicia); (3) cruelty and unbrotherly conduct (Edom,
Moab). If the Moab part of the cycle is viewed as transi-
tional to the indictment of Judah, the charges begin and end
with cruelty in war; and the emphasis is upon enslaving
fellow human beings.

Is it not possible to see all three of these elements as
complementary to Amos' purpose? Certainly there is *geographical arrangement.* The events surely have historical

interconnections. Also, there is a strong ethical reason for including the *denunciations*. They lay a strong basis for the *condemnation* of Israel's offenses. These aspects are so intertwined as to defy separation. They all add to the climactic impact as Israel was brought face to face with her own sins.

Notice the careful framework in which the accusations are couched. The literary formula "three . . . four transgressions" prefaces each indictment. The formula probably meant "for more than enough transgressions." One instance of the nations' guilt is then given by way of example. Finally, punishment and promise of destruction are set forth. Each indictment thus begins with similar wording and ends in almost identical terms. It is obvious that Amos had a purposeful plan which he carried through to careful completion.

II. The Charges Against Israel's Neighbors (1:3 to 2:3)

The idea of one nation condemning another is as old as recorded history. The modern counterpart can be seen in a White Paper issued by one nation against another. The purpose is usually twofold: to accuse the other nation of specific acts of misconduct and to justify its own pattern of international behavior. Amos accused the other nations of misconduct, but he refused to paint a white picture for Israel.

1. *Damascus* (1:3–5)

The city of Damascus stood as the epitome of the entire national life of Aram, or Syria. As the capital of the kingdom, it set the tone of behavior for all the nation. The Syrian kingdom, lying to the northeast of Israel, was strategically located along the major trade routes of antiquity. This people, conquered by David, regained independence during the latter part of Solomon's reign. Until the time of Amos, the Syrians were the most persistent and dangerous foe to Israel.

(1) *The charge.*—Although Syria was greatly weakened when Amos spoke at Bethel, the atrocities of former years were well remembered. In fact, many of the people who heard Amos could have filled in the remaining charges to round out the three or four transgressions.

The best remembered atrocities were associated with the names of King Hazael and his son Benhadad III, when they attacked the Israelites of Gilead to the east of the Jordan River. (See 2 Kings 8:12; 10:32–33; 13:3, 7.) Amos singled out an act of cruelty contrary to all standards of decency—dragging threshing instruments of iron over the bodies of the Gileadites. These implements were made from planks of wood spiked with iron or basalt fragments. While Amos' charge may refer to an actual incident of torture, it may also be used figuratively to sum up the many atrocities of Hazael and Benhadad.

(2) *The punishment.*—The certainty of punishment is brought out at the beginning and end of each cycle. In the introductory formula (1:3) the word for punishment is not in the Hebrew. The verse reads literally, "and for four, I will not turn *it* away." "It" may refer to God's anger, hand, decree, word, or punishment. (See Amos 1:6, 9, 11, 13; 2:1, 4, 6.) However, the idea of punishment is so clear as to lead many translators to insert the word "punishment" in each of the above references. In *The Book of Amos,* E. A. Edghill has suggested that the revisers might "have given a more impressive rendering if they had restored the solemn yet vaguely terrifying 'it' of the original."

Amos described various methods of punishment for Damascus (1:4–5). Fire signified the ravages from the flame of war. The "bar of Damascus" referred to the method of securing the gate of a walled city. The cutting off of inhabitants from their place of refuge would end in the Syrians being carried captive back to Kir, their place of origin. The mention of specific kings and places gave an added note of realism to the stark devastation to come.

2. *Gaza* (1:6–8)

Gaza was one of the five ruling cities among the Philistines. It held a place of strong leadership in the nation. Philistia and Israel had been traditional enemies since the time of the judges, when these sea peoples settled in mass along the Mediterranean coast to the southeast of Israel. Their position along the coastal caravan route brought them into contact with many peoples. Gaza thus became the emporium of trade from the north, south, and the desert regions.

(1) *The charge.*—Many were the atrocities to which Amos might have appealed. Again, he chose one as representative of the inhumanity of the Philistines: the selling into slavery of a whole town or district. It was a part of the universal ancient practice to carry captive and even sell peoples taken in war. However, the Philistines offended the public conscience by raiding villages without the excuse of war, selling complete or peaceful communities as a commercial enterprise. They had thus become the source of a slave-trading ring in which the Edomites were the middlemen, taking the slaves to other markets for resale.

(2) *The punishment.*—In addition to Gaza as the slave-trading emporium, three other ruling cities of the Philistines —Ashdod, Ashkelon, and Ekron—were singled out for denunciation. Judgments upon Philistia were similar to those for Damascus. The passage leaves little doubt that the name of the Philistines would be blotted out.

3. *Tyre* (1:9-10)

The city of Tyre represented the extensive coastal kingdom of the Phoenicians, northwest of Israel. As the most important and the greatest commercial center, she typified the best and the worst in the Phoenician culture. Since the people were primarily merchants, artisans, and sailors, her relations with Israel and other neighbors were basically peaceful. Tyrian workmen had aided in the building programs of David and Solomon. Tyre was also known to the Israelites through Jezebel, daughter of the king of Tyre, who became queen of Israel.

(1) *The charge.*—Amos brought a new complaint in regard to Tyre—the way they failed to remember "the covenant of brotherhood" (1:9, RSV). The reference may have been to the covenant David and Solomon had made with Hiram some three hundred years earlier. However, the prophet was probably referring to the way in which Tyre

broke her treaty with her sister cities and callously sold
fellow Phoenicians into slavery. This interpretation reveals
Amos' concern about the rights of all humanity, as well as
about mistreatment of God's people.

(2) *The punishment.*—The overthrow of Tyre by fire was
threatened. Such a destruction was also predicted in the
writings of Isaiah, Ezekiel, and Zechariah. However, because of Tyre's ready willingness to pay tribute to would-be
conquerers, her destruction was not realized until 332 B.C.,
when Alexander the Great captured the city after a siege
of seven months.

4. Edom (1:11-12)

Amos next shifted his attacks from cities representing nations to three nations or tribal groups. Edom was a kingdom
of seminomadic and nomadic people who lived to the southeast of Judah and south of the Dead Sea. Their close kinship
to the Israelites was evident in their traditional origin from
Esau, brother of Jacob. Warfare against Edom was for-
bidden to the Israelites during the journey to the land of
Canaan. Caleb and other Edomites joined the Israelites in
the conquest and settlement. However, under David the
people of Edom lost their independence to the Israelites
and were kept under bondage for two centuries. After fifty
years of independence, they were again made subject to
Judah.

(1) *The charge.*—Since Edom was more closely related
to Israel than to any other neighbor, brotherly feelings
should have been respected. It was not just an act of which
Amos spoke; it was a state of mind and spirit that nurtured
the hatred which had developed. Not only did Edom's anger
tear within, but she cherished her wrath and nursed it along
(v. 11). Instead of letting time heal the wounds, the Edomites brooded, waiting for the moment of revenge.

(2) *The punishment.*—Again the punishment is singu-
larly that of fire and the attendant ravages of war (v. 12).
The district of Teman was probably in the northern part of
Edom, taking its name from an Edomite clan mentioned in

Genesis 36:11,15. It should also be recalled that Eliphaz, one of Job's friends, was described as a Temanite (Job 2:11). The stronghold of Bozrah represented the towns and Teman the rural districts in this picture of coming disaster.

5. *Ammon* (1:13–15)

A kinship also existed between Ammon and Israel, since both the Ammonites and Moabites were traditionally regarded as descendants of Lot, Abraham's nephew (Gen. 19: 36–38). These nomadic people lived east of the Jordan along the fringe of the desert. Since the time of the judges, they had been a harassing threat to the Israelites in Transjordan. Although David subjugated them, control was weak or nonexistent after the death of Solomon.

(1) *The charge.*—Here Amos made his accusation of Ammon's barbarous act. Although many recoil in horror today at the thought of pregnant women ripped apart by invaders, this was apparently not uncommon in ancient warfare. (See 2 Kings 8:12; 15:16; Hos. 13:16.) Amos showed the added inhumanity of the deed by mentioning that the purpose was no more than greedy desire for more land. There were no circumstances of self-defense or ancient blood revenge—only wanton cruelty and cold-blooded atrocity.

(2) *The punishment.*—The indignation of Amos toward the crimes of the Ammonites was matched by the lengthy description of their destruction. The ravages of war were pictured by fire, the shouts of advancing foes, and the storming of the city. The tempest and whirlwind were figurative expressions to describe the onslaught as having the effect of a hurricane. Again, Amos mentioned the captivity of the king, adding the princes to the list of the vanquished.

6. *Moab* (2:1–3)

The Moabites lived on the then fertile tableland east of the Dead Sea. As already mentioned, they were closely linked with the Ammonites and the Israelites, both linguistically and historically. The Moabite kingdom was conquered by David, but gained independence at the death of Solomon.

The country again became subjects of the Northern Kingdom under Omri. However, it returned to an independent status during the reign of Ahab.

(1) *The charge.*—Many are the sordid acts of war which have come down from antiquity. Among the worst for the ancients was the disrespect and defilement of the tomb of their king. Amos spoke with a universal conscience in condemning the irreverent burning of the bones of the king of Edom. This unbridled outrage called forth cries of revenge from Edomites and foreigners alike.

(2) *The punishment.*—The symbol of a dying nation was used by Amos to picture the end for Moab. The fire, uproar, shouting, and trumpet would be picturesque terms, well remembered by all who had been a part of the siege of a city. The end would soon come for the kings, the princes, and the cities. In fact, after the exile nothing was heard from Moab again. The name became a geographical term rather than the designation of a proud nation.

III. The Indictment of God's People (2:4-16)

At this point in his sermon Amos had created an air of excitement, charged with enthusiasm. The crowds must have wondered where he would turn next. They had undoubtedly expressed their enthusiasm in various ways. All had reached a high pitch of frenzied approval. Then Amos struck fire with his condemnation of his own homeland Judah.

1. *Judah* (2:4-5)

Since the division of the kingdom (about 922 B.C.), Judah and Israel had been off and on again in their relationships as friend and foe. Some people in each kingdom no doubt liked the separate arrangement and learned to speak disparagingly of the other nation. Others continued to maintain brotherly ties and hoped for the day when the glories of David's kingdom would be realized again. Jerusalem remained a religious rallying point with distinct historic connections.

(1) *The charge.*—It was evident in Amos' day that Judah had in essence already rejected the teaching of the Lord by failing to remain faithful to his commandments. The prophet probably had already laid this charge at Judah's doorstep. That Amos had in mind the spiritual and moral teachings, rather than mere ceremonial ordinances, was made apparent by the insistence with which he emphasized moral duties. The "lies" which "caused them to err" may well have been the false gods after which their fathers had walked. The charge given here cuts through to the heart of Judah's problem. The brevity of the indictment may well be due to the inclusion of Judah in later messages under the term "house of Israel."

(2) *The punishment.*—Judah is not pictured as escaping the fiery destruction to come. No miracle is promised to stem the tide of the invader. Even Jerusalem, the Holy City, comes under the indictment. A sense of equality in judgment is manifested in the use of the same figure for Judah as employed for the heathen nations.

2. *Israel* (2:6–16)

At last Amos came to his unforgettable climax, the point toward which he had been moving. His audience had agreed repeatedly that punishment must come to the outsiders for their atrocious offenses against recognized principles of morality. They had shown their approval of punishment for Judah, which had sinned against the teachings of God. Now Amos must carry this recognition of deserved punishment to the very heart of Israel, which had sinned against love—the type of love both demonstrated and taught by the righteous God. In effect, Israel had already passed judgment on herself by accepting the validity of Amos' argument that Judah and the other nations must stand condemned.

(1) *The charges* (2:6–12).—Amos opened with the same formula which he had used for the other rebuked nations: "For three transgressions of Israel, and for four." However, instead of choosing one offense as illustrative, he pointed out

four which serve to demonstrate the true character of Israel's national life. These are the basic charges found throughout the book.

Corruption of justice was Amos' first count in the indictment against Israel (2:6). The "righteous" were probably those whom we would call the "innocent." These were pronounced guilty by bribed judges. This same indictment was voiced by Isaiah, Micah, and Ezekiel. These innocent ones were "sold out" by unjust and partial judges. The second phrase is seemingly parallel in thought to the first, referring again to the selling of the unfortunate. Scholars are divided as to the type of selling involved. The reference may be to the selling of justice by corrupt judges or the selling into slavery by greedy creditors who took advantage of a legal judgment. The phrase, "for a pair of shoes," was a striking proverbial saying which probably parallels our expression about selling something "for a song"—for a trifling sum.

Oppression of the poor was the second count brought by Amos (2:7a). The most obvious connection of "the dust of the earth on the head of the poor" is with the practice of putting dust on one's head as a sign of mourning or misfortune. However, this probably referred to a desire to see dust on the heads of the poor, in order to rejoice in their misfortune. The Revised Standard Version uses an interesting paraphrase which describes the oppressors as trampling the head of the poor. The second phrase, "and turn aside the way of the meek," points to those who placed hindrances in the way of helpless but humble servants of God in order to thwart their purpose.

Immorality in the name of religion was a third count against Amos' hearers (2:7b). He had observed the people who went into the places of worship to engage in the sacred prostitution rites copied from the Canaanites. How revolting it must have been for Amos to see fathers and sons going in for such perversion of life and worship. Under Manasseh, king of Judah, this practice was followed in the precincts of the Temple at Jerusalem. Such acts could do nothing less than profane the very name of God!

Self-indulgence rounds out the list of counts mentioned in the indictment by Amos (2:8). Using the clothing taken in pledge as something to lie upon and drinking the wine taken as fines are actions which further illustrate the depths to which Israel had fallen. The former refers to clothing pawned by debtors; the latter relates to wine collected by priests or judges as fines for civil or ceremonial judgments. Whether these two deeds have a relation to the acts of immorality in 2:7 or concern events during feasts is not clear. Whatever the occasion, the place is "by every altar" and "in the house of their god."

The charge of ingratitude was yet another accusation which Amos added, while contrasting sharply God's favor and leadership with the response of ingratitude on the part of Israel. Four evidences of God's mighty acts and merciful deeds presented his case: God's destruction of the inhabitants of Canaan, his leadership of Israel out of bondage and through the wilderness, his calling forth of prophets, and his raising up Nazirites. The prophets served to announce God's will, and the Nazirites lived as godly examples before the people. Yet, instead of gratefully receiving God's blessings, the Israelites commanded the prophets to keep silent and made the Nazirites break their vows concerning abstinence from strong drink. How insensible to the richest spiritual resources were these men who would silence the ones sent from God and compromise the witness of the ones especially dedicated to exemplary living!

(2) *The punishment* (2:13-16).—The visitation of God was again pictured as a battle scene, yet without the metaphors previously employed. Although the idea of utter disaster is obvious, the exact meaning of the figure of speech in 2:13 is obscure. Either the pressure of a loaded cart or the tottering of the earth beneath such a cart is used to describe Israel's future discomfort.

Since the strong or mighty warrior, the skilled archer, the swift runner, the expert horseman, and the courageous fighter would be unable to stand in that day, what chance has the ordinary man? In full retreat, all will throw off weapons, dress, and everything which might hinder flight and "flee away naked" (v. 16). The chapters which follow elaborate further on the nature of Israel's fate.

IV. CONCLUSION

The approach used by Amos should be thoughtfully examined by every preacher and teacher today. Many are the onetime visitors in our churches who are not challenged to come back again. In some way they were not really involved in the sermon or lesson. We have failed to gain their sympathetic attention. We have not been able to demand identification of the hearers with the Christ whom we proclaim. Both applied psychology and purposeful planning are essential for the one who would share the message of God with those of our day.

In this age of rapid communication and transportation, national boundaries are giving way to international concern. This is a time for Christians to speak out against the atrocities daily committed in many parts of the world. Cruelty in war, the enslaving of peoples, the disregard of treaty obligations, unbrotherly conduct, and inhuman treatment of peoples are still offenses against universally recognized principles of morality. These sins of barbarism and the attendant absence of pity are subjects upon which the followers of Christ have too long been silent. Amos would point Christians to the God-given task as spokesmen for God among the nations.

Since sin is not limited to those outside the people of God, our task must include attention to the "inside" sins. The Christian conscience must be made more aware of the sins of injustice, oppression, immorality, and self-indulgence. At the heart of all such sins against God's teachings and God's love is still a sense of ingratitude in which we demonstrate an oblivion to the manifold blessings of God. There are still those who would silence the prophet in our midst and compromise the person trying to live an exemplary life. Truly the words of Amos speak to this age, to a culture in which God's love is as much desecrated as it ever was in ancient Israel. In

the words of Jesus, "He that hath ears to hear, let him hear"
(Matt. 11:15).

FOR CLASS PREPARATION

1. Look up in a Bible dictionary each of the peoples mentioned
by Amos, in order to understand better their background and
history.
2. Watch your daily paper during the time of this course for
examples of cruel, heartless, and unbrotherly acts which parallel *in principle* those described by Amos. Clip and bring to
class the best examples.
3. Check as many references in the Bible as possible which show
contacts between Israel and the other nations referred to by
Amos. (See list below.)

FOR ADVANCED STUDY

1. For more discussion of Amos' method of approach:
G. A. Smith, *The Book of the Twelve Prophets,* I, 119–122.
2. For further understanding of Amos' use of "law" in 2:4:
R. S. Cripps, *The Book of Amos,* pp. 284–286.
S. R. Driver, *Joel and Amos* (Cambridge Bible), pp. 230–231.
3. For a better picture of the life of the Nazirite (2:11–12):
R. L. Honeycutt, *Amos and His Message,* pp. 46–47.
S. H. Hooke, "Nazirite," *Dictionary of the Bible* (Hastings), rev. ed.
by F. C. Grant and H. H. Rowley, pp. 691–692.
4. For background contact between Israel and other nations:
Damascus (Syrians)—2 Samuel 8:5–6; 10:15–19; 1 Kings 11:
23–25; 20:26–30; 22:29–37; 2 Kings 14:28; 16:5–9; Isaiah
17:1–3; Jeremiah 49:23–27.
Gaza (Philistines)—Joshua 13:1–3; Judges 16:18–21; 1 Samuel 5:
10–11; 31:1ff; 2 Samuel 5:22–25; Zephaniah 2:4–7; Jeremiah
47:1–7; Zechariah 9:5–7.
Tyre (Phoenicians)—2 Samuel 5:11–12; 1 Kings 5:1–12; 1 Kings
7:13–14; 9:10–14; Isaiah 23:1ff; Zechariah 9:3–4; Joel 3:4–8.
Edom (Edomites)—Genesis 25:30; 36:1–8; Numbers 20:14–21;
2 Samuel 8:13–14; 2 Kings 8:20–22; Jeremiah 49:17–22; Ezekiel
25:12–14; Malachi 1:4–5.
Ammon (Ammonites)—Genesis 19:36–38; Judges 11:4ff; 1 Samuel
11:1–11; 2 Samuel 10:9–14; Isaiah 11:11–16; Zephaniah 2:
8–11; Jeremiah 49:1–6.
Moab (Moabites)—Genesis 19:36–37; Numbers 22:1–6; 24:17;
Deuteronomy 34:5; 2 Samuel 8:1–2; 2 Kings 3:4–8, 26–27;
Isaiah 15:1ff; Zephaniah 2:8–11; Jeremiah 48.

CHAPTER 4

THE HAZARDS OF PRIVILEGE—AMOS 3

I. ISRAEL'S UNIQUE POSITION (3:1–2a)
1. The Principle of Election
2. The Covenant Relationship

II. ISRAEL'S EXTRAORDINARY RESPONSIBILITY (3:2b–8)
1. A Startling Conclusion (3:2b)
2. Revealed Through Prophetic Insight (3:3–8)

III. ISRAEL'S SPECIAL PENALTY (3:9–15)
1. A Call for Witnesses (3:9–10)
2. A Promise of Certain Destruction (3:11–15)

4

The Hazards of Privilege

AMOS 3

WHAT RANKS A PEOPLE as outstanding in world history? What qualities in a nation destine it to occupy a favored place in the affairs of men? Easy answers to such questions are impossible. Surely geographical location, natural resources, available leadership, and ability of the people all play an important part in bringing a nation to prominence. The relative power and ability of contemporary nations are vital factors. Yet, all of these factors appear secondary when the history of ancient Israel is examined. Something else must explain the dynamic of this people of long ago.

I. ISRAEL'S UNIQUE POSITION (3:1–2a)

It was never the desire of God's people, Israel, to become "part and parcel" with surrounding nations. There was a distinctiveness inherent in her thinking and corporate personality. While at many stages in Israel's history the mass of the people may have forgotten their uniqueness, a rich heritage was always there to call them back to God. This heritage constantly reminded them of the promises made to Abraham, Moses, and their successors. Such phrases as "a peculiar people," "a holy nation," and "a holy priesthood" served as guidelines in maintaining their distinctiveness.

1. *The Principle of Election*

Amos did not seek any natural explanation for Israel's place in history but looked to her special place in the economy of God's purpose. At first glance the statement, "You only have I known of all the families of the earth" (3:2), would seem to narrow greatly the concern of God for his creation and to limit his knowledge of the world. However, the restriction or limitation did not rule out concern for the other nations of the world; it involved a sense of election for Israel as an instrument of God's will. The type of knowledge which Amos had in mind was a personal, intimate knowledge devoid of discrimination but filled with experiential understanding. The psalmist used the same word when he stated, "The Lord knoweth the way of the righteous" (Psalm 1:6). In a very special way God knew Israel in deep experience and abiding love.

(1) *The element of choice.*—The Old Testament makes clear that Israel was regarded as the Chosen People of God. They were chosen for a ministry of service. This was not automatically a predestination to eternal salvation. This very element of choice on God's part involved his right to revoke the original decision. Even though God had made the choice, he was still the sovereign Lord who could alter his original plan. Inherent in God's choice of Israel was the prospect of judgment whenever his people failed to measure up to their high calling.

A deep sense of being chosen as a unique people was set forth in the book of Deuteronomy:

> For you are a people holy to the Lord your God; the Lord your God has chosen you to be a people for his own possession, out of all the peoples that are on the face of the earth. It was not because you were more in number than any other people that the Lord set his love upon you and chose you, for you were the fewest of all peoples; but it is because the Lord loves you, and is keeping the oath which he swore to your fathers, that the Lord has brought you out with a mighty hand, and redeemed you from the house of bondage, from the hand of Pharaoh king of Egypt.
>
> —7:6–8, RSV

It should be noted that the prophets invariably linked the exodus from Egypt with God's choice of Israel. While the call of Abraham was viewed as a distinct break with the past, Abraham was more of a forerunner from whom the

Chosen People sprang. The Exodus experience was the hub around which Israel's self-realization revolved. As Hosea said, "When Israel was a child, then I loved him, and called my son out of Egypt" (Hos. 11:1).

(2) *The element of grace.*—In no way had the Israelites earned their calling from God. Just as Amos gave no natural explanation of Israel's uniqueness, he claimed no justification based upon merit. Nothing short of God's grace could explain how Israel had been privileged as the first nation to know God in his act of self-revelation. No Old Testament writer makes the claim that the nation's inherent greatness led God to choose Israel. Rather the opposite is taught: that Israel's greatness lay in God's unmerited favor in choosing her.

2. *The Covenant Relationship*

The election of Israel was made more concrete by the bond of covenant between God and his people. This covenant was established between God and his people at Sinai. (See Ex. 19.) The idea of covenant was used to explain the meaning and nature of Israel's election. The symbol was borrowed from the realm of law and given a theological application. The basic idea of covenant between individuals was present in the stories of David and Jonathan (1 Sam. 18:3; 20:8; 23:18), as well as Jacob and Laban (Gen. 31: 44–55). Likewise there were covenants or treaties between sovereign rulers and subjects which provided interesting parallels to the practices in Israel.

However, God's covenant was more than an idea or a means of explaining divine-human relationships. The concept took form as an enactment of a spiritual reality. In patriarchal days there was the ceremony of cutting an animal in half and walking between the two parts (Gen. 15:9–18). Later it took the form of a covenant renewal ceremony. The people would again accept the conditions of the covenant, ratifying the terms for their own generation. (See Ex. 24:1–8; Josh. 24:15–27; Deut. 29.)

The principle involved in covenant responsibility was

mutual loyalty and obligation between two parties not related by blood ties. The key word came to be faithfulness, expressed by the Hebrew concept of God's love within the covenant. It was through this deep love that God and people were bound together in the covenant. Behind it all was the sense of election by which Israel was chosen to be a blessing to the world.

II. ISRAEL'S EXTRAORDINARY RESPONSIBILITY (3:2b–8)

Amos appealed to the nationalistic tendencies in Israel by his premise, "You only have I known . . ." In fact, this may well have been the answer given by some of Amos' hearers to the message recorded in Amos 1–2. The people probably expressed their approval and expected Amos to continue, "therefore I will bless you abundantly." After all, did not their wealth prove that God loved them greatly?

1. A Startling Conclusion (3:2b)

Although Amos was perfectly willing to accept the idea of special status for Israel among the nations, he was unwilling to accept the expected conclusion. Instead, the prophet thundered out with, "Therefore I will punish you for all your iniquities." What a twist of meaning to drive home the message of certain punishment! While the people of Israel thought that their privileged place in the election-covenant plans of God meant only further blessing, Amos was even more certain that it meant judgment for failure to remain faithful.

At the heart of Amos' conviction was the insight that privilege invariably brings responsibility. The Israelites were actually denying their obligation of responsibility. They were saying that it did not really matter what they did nor how they lived. God would take care of them anyway. The majority of the people of Israel developed an air of superiority, tending to consider themselves in a different class from the other nations.

Lest we become as complacent as the Israelites, it would be good to look at the parable of the talents used by Jesus.

Just as much was required of Israel, so is even more required of those privileged with the gospel message. Interpreting the parable for his disciples, Jesus said: "Every one to whom much is given, of him will much be required; and of him to whom men commit much they will demand the more" (Luke 12:48, RSV). Far too many Christians claim the same immunity and superiority as did Israel of Amos' day, appealing to a distorted understanding of the phrase, "once saved, always saved." Privilege is no less accompanied by responsibility now than it was in the days of Amos or Jesus. The practice of religious acts is no insurance against the judgment of God. Mere activism is no substitute for the acceptance of genuine responsibility toward God and fellowman. Privilege involves opportunity, not escapism. Immunity cannot be claimed simply because of past favor of God, irrespective of deeds and the measure of faithful service. The dominant position of Christianity in America is not assured as irrevocable because we have always enjoyed a favored status. Being favorably known by God lays upon us a dreadful but thrilling responsibility to be found faithful in our stewardship.

2. *Revealed Through Prophetic Insight* (3:3–8)

As logical as Amos' argument appears, many who heard him were quick to deny the validity of his words. The boom economy, the military victories, and the sense of security seemed contrary to the whole argument advanced by the prophet. He appeared to be presenting a theory not supported by the observable facts. However, Amos had a grasp of facts not discernible to the average person of his day. His insight into the realm of international affairs reached far beyond the political leaders. His spiritual understanding surpassed the work of prophet and priest alike.

Amos proceeded to answer unrecorded objections by means of illustrations drawn from everyday life, a pattern later to be used by Jesus himself in the Sermon on the Mount. Amos recognized that there was a cause operative behind every event or occurrence. He was not willing to write off as "fate" or "chance" the things which mystified the average man. With keen insight Amos looked behind the event for the cause which produced it. It should be obvious that the questions raised were rhetorical and that a negative answer was expected.

(1) *Illustrations from the wilderness* (3:3–5).—Amos began with man's relation with man, implying that two men do not walk together unless they have reached some agreement to do so. This would be especially true of those who met within the wild regions where Amos had grown up. The Septuagint (early Greek translation of the Old Testament) has an interesting translation, suggesting that two men will not walk together "except they know each other." In the preceding verse it is Israel whom God has intimately "known." Surely the reference is to the lack of agreement between Israel and God, since the covenant relation implies a deep sense of agreement on covenant obligations.

Amos drew further upon his wilderness experiences, remembering vividly the ominous forebodings of his shepherd life. He knew well how the lion keeps silent until he leaps on his prey. Only then is his roar heard. The young lion growls in delight only when his hunger is about to be satisfied by food. The wild bird does not become ensnared in a hunter's net unless there is bait to attract him, nor do the folds of the net spring up unless there is a bird for the net to enclose. Amos was probably pointing to Assyria as the lion about to pounce on his prey and as the hunter who had already set the trap for the blind and unsuspecting Israel.

2. *Illustrations from city life* (3:6).—Although Amos was most at home in the desert regions, he was quite familiar with the problems of cities under siege. He had already pictured the punishments to come upon the nations as related to military conquest. Again he used the familiar warning of the trumpet sound to remind the people of the fear which they should already feel. Such a warning sound had the same power to send chills along the spine of the ancient as an air raid siren in the middle of night for modern man.

Amos went still deeper in picturing the cause of calamity upon a city as he saw the hand of God behind the event. The idea of God causing "evil" was consistent with the Old Testament concept of God. (See 1 Kings 9:9; 2 Kings 21:12.) However, the idea behind the word translated "evil" involved physical, not moral, evil. The concept is better conveyed by the word "calamity."

Amos thus presented the failure of Israel in her covenant agreement with God. He saw God about to send calamity upon his people. The prophet stood amazed at the blind leaders leading a blind people who could not read the signs of the times. He could not understand why they did not tremble at the judgment about to come.

(3) *The certainty: God has spoken* (3:7-8).—The foregoing illustrations were used to indicate the type of authority which Amos claimed. These were not the words of a seer gazing into his crystal ball nor the product of a soothsayer's devices. Herein was the insight of a true prophet who saw signs around him and recognized the significance of these events.

G. A. Smith clearly pointed out the manner of revelation asserted by Amos, when he wrote:

> The prophet is thus made sure of his message by the agreement between the inward convictions of his soul and the outward events of the day. When these walk together, it proves that they have come of a common purpose. He who causes the events—it is God Himself, *for shall there be calamity in a city and Yahweh not have done it?*—must be author also of the inner voice or conviction which agrees with them. *Who* then *can but prophesy?* Observe again that no support is here derived from miracle; nor is claim made for the prophet on the ground of his ability to foretell the event. It is the agreement of the idea with the fact, their evident common origin in the purpose of God, which makes a man sure that he has in him the Word of God. Both are necessary, and together are enough.[1]

It was through such men as Amos that the secret counsel of God was revealed to Israel (v. 7). No one could claim that God had acted capriciously, since he had warned them through the prophets. Certainly Amos had in mind the revelation of matters of utmost importance for Israel, not minute details of God's providential care within human history. At the time of each great crisis in Israel's history, the Lord called forth a prophet, or prophets, to meet the emergency and warn the people. Many of these probably shared the conviction with Amos: "The lion hath roared, who will not fear? the Lord God hath spoken, who can but prophesy?" (3:8). These men found their interpretation of events from an inner conviction that God had spoken.

Do not these principles still apply today in the working out of God's purposes through his servants? It is not through the multiplicity of experiences or the detailed knowledge of history that God's will is realized. The prophet today must be certain that the inner convictions laid upon his heart coincide with the outward events which evidence the movement of God within human history. Once the message is clear, he, too, can say with Amos: "The Lord God hath spoken, who can but prophesy?"

III. ISRAEL'S SPECIAL PENALTY (3:9–15)

In the light of Israel's stubbornness and unfaithful conduct toward God, Amos saw judgment as inevitable. Never did he waver in this conviction which had been so indelibly impressed upon his heart. It was not the secret desire of a jealous prophet nor a determination that his message be vindicated. Amos could see no alternative in the light of Israel's past actions and present attitudes.

1. A Call for Witnesses (3:9–10)

Amos called Israel to an unusual scene in which enemy nations were invited to view judgment at the capital city of Samaria. The hill upon which the city was located was one of the most imposing in Palestine. Surrounded by a vast valley of level ground beyond which were hills on every side, the setting was ideal. The city represented well the wealth, position, and prestige of the nation. All of the sins which Amos condemned were very much present in this outstanding but corrupt city.

(1) *Appeal to the common conscience of humanity.*—It was not Amos' desire to ridicule the people of God but to apply the same type of reasoning which he had used in the opening chapters of his book. Just as he had pictured the outspoken sins and atrocities of outsiders, he sought the verdict of others in regard to Israel.

How demoralizing this device must have seemed to the hearers of Amos' message! Many may well have been infuriated at the thought of calling in their enemies to conduct an examination. However, Israel's sins had reached the point where even the heathen nations must recognize the necessity of judgment. The degree of Israel's blindness to her own sin was graphically presented by the necessity of calling in those outside the covenant relation.

There is not complete agreement as to which nations were called as judges. The King James Version follows the Hebrew reading, referring to Ashdod (Philistia) and Egypt. The Revised Standard Version follows the Septuagint, mentioning Assyria and Egypt. Regardless of the translation you accept, the two groups named are representative of all the heathen nations.

(2) *The basis of condemnation.*—Amos here pictured Israel in a state of confusion and disorder. Might and oppression were ruling over right and justice. Such a condition had come about, not by sheer chance, but because "they know not to do right" (3:10). No longer did they desire that which was true, straightforward, and honest. Amos was setting in sharp contrast the way of God's teaching with the way of robbery and violence. The rulers and leaders were guilty of extreme forms of oppression, storing up their ill-gotten gains in their palaces.

Hosea condemned the same type of oppression and attributed it to a similar lack of understanding, saying: "My people are destroyed for lack of knowledge: because thou hast rejected knowledge, I will also reject thee, that thou shalt be no priest to me: seeing thou hast forgotten the law of thy God, I will also forget thy children" (Hos. 4:6). The sin of Israel was not some specific unpardonable act; it was the state of mind and attitude of life which left her without the power of moral discernment.

The words of Amos had not penetrated far into the society of Israel. Yet, with almost two thousand years of light from the teachings of Jesus, our society is still characterized by a similar rejection of knowledge—the knowledge derived from the totality of God's revelation to men. Our nation constantly is being judged in terms of our Christian claims as well as upon the scales of the common conscience of humanity. Can we honestly demonstrate twenty-seven hundred years of progress and growth over the Israel of Amos' day?

2. A Promise of Certain Destruction (3:11-15)

The word "therefore" strongly introduces the conclusion which must be drawn from the evidence submitted. An unidentified enemy, probably Assyria, would crash through and pull down the defenses of the proud city of Samaria. The palaces, already called storehouses of violence and robbery, would be despoiled. The terse description of devastation in verse 11 points to a complete and certain destruction which must have raised the question among Amos' listeners, Will not some escape?

(1) An element of hope.—Amos seems to have replied that there would be a glimmer of hope. Yet, his answer barely modified the original picture of utter doom. Using again the figures of lion, sheep, and shepherd—so much a part of his daily life in the wilderness of Tekoa—Amos spoke of the remnant left after a lion's attack. The two shinbones and a piece of an ear represented all that remained for the shepherd to take home. (According to Exodus 22:13, the parts of an animal left by an attacking beast must be brought to the owner to prove the shepherd's claim.) Israel was likened to the destroyed sheep, with only a small remnant left behind.

The illustration by Amos did not give a great deal of consolation. It was not at all likely to turn a pessimist into

an optimist. However, the very idea of a remnant spoke
an important message concerning the mercy of God. Amos
returned to this theme later.

(2) *Examples of destruction.*—Along with the devastation of Samaria would come other visitation of God's judgment. Especially pointed is the reference to the royal
sanctuaries at Bethel. That the altars, defiled by practices
of heresy should be torn down is no surprise. Amos' several
rebukes of superficial worship would point to the tearing
down of these symbols of substitute worship. The major
sting of the prophet's words concerned the cutting off of the
horns of the altar. These horns were artificial projections
from each corner, probably resembling originally the horns
of an ox. Their purpose related to the right of sanctuary for
one fleeing from an oppressor or enemy. Such a person was,
under law, regarded as safe when he gained entry to the
sanctuary and took hold of the horns. Amos thus pointed
out that there would be no sense of sanctuary for those who
attempt to flee in the day of God's judgment upon Israel.

Amos' last example of destruction concerned the houses,
of which the rich were quite proud. He displayed his indignation toward these evidences of unbridled luxury and
prosperity by mentioning such houses four times (v. 15).
Coming from the austerity of the desert, where a tent or
the open air was his home, the prophet was more aware of
these symbols of gross materialism. He was concerned about
the sharp contrast between the extreme poverty of the
underprivileged and the opulence of the rich. Even further,
he was anxious about the false foundation upon which the
society was built.

The "winter house with the summer house" was probably
a two-story structure with special facilities for summer living
in the upper story. The "houses of ivory" were those embel-
lished with ivory inlaid panels. The "great houses" may have
been large palaces, or the phrase may be translated "the
many houses," referring to a multiplicity of houses owned
by one person or family. These were a sign of excessive
luxury in the time of Amos. They served as an illustration

of the selfishness and greed of those who cared not that others were going hungry in their land.

The application of these observations by Amos is too obvious for comfort in relation to our society today. E. A. Edghill has captured something of Amos' boldness as he has written:

> We, no less than ancient Israel, are far too much inclined to accept the sins of civilization as the normal state of affairs. After the feeblest of protests, we acquiesce in social conditions irreconcilable with any Christian standard; we regard them as inevitable, as a regrettable necessity. We need a prophet like Amos to come forward, and call these things by their proper names; and in answer to our plausible pretexts to declare that, if these things are an essential part of our social system, then God will Himself deal with the whole matter in such a way that the downfall of the system will be irretrievable. It is the prophet's task *to challenge contemporary civilization in the name of God;* to insist, as Amos insisted, that no price is too high to pay for social righteousness.[3]

FOR CLASS PREPARATION

1. Compare the following references to Israel's unique position: Genesis 17:4-8; 18:18-19; 46:3; Exodus 19:5-6; Deuteronomy 7:6-11; 14:2, 21; Hosea 11:1-4; Jeremiah 2:2-3.
2. Make a list of ways in which we, as the people of God, have a unique sense of privilege today. Compare these evidences of special favor with those of ancient Israel.
3. Consider seriously the demands of responsibility and faithfulness arising out of our covenant relation with God through Christ. (See Matt. 25:14-30; Luke 12:42-48; 16:10-13.)

FOR ADVANCED STUDY

1. For a more detailed discussion of Israel's election by God: John Bright, *The Kingdom of God,* pp. 27-30, 63-64.
   R. S. Cripps, *The Book of Amos,* pp. 334-335.
   H. H. Rowley, *The Biblical Doctrine of Election,* pp. 15-94.
2. For further consideration of the covenant relation:

James Barr, "Covenant," *Dictionary of the Bible* (Hastings), Rev. Ed. by F. C. Grant and H. H. Rowley, pp. 183–185.

G. E. Mendenhall, "Covenant," *The Interpreter's Dictionary of the Bible*, A–D, 714–723.

Norman Snaith, *The Distinctive Ideas of the Old Testament*, pp. 107ff.

3. For a closer examination of prophetic insight:

Otto Baab, *Prophetic Preaching*, pp. 84–106.

A. B. Davidson, *Old Testament Prophecy*, pp. 144–158.

J. M. Gettys, *Hark to the Trumpet*, pp. 57–75.

H. W. Robinson, *Inspiration and Revelation*, pp. 173–186.

R. B. Y. Scott, *The Relevance of the Prophets*, pp. 84–103.

---

[1] G. A. Smith, *The Book of the Twelve Prophets* (rev. ed.; New York: Harper & Row Publishers, 1928), I, 89.

[2] Edghill, *The Book of Amos* (2nd ed.; London: Methuen and Co., 1926), pp. 33–34.

CHAPTER 5

INEVITABLE JUDGMENT—AMOS 4

I. UNLIMITED CORRUPTION (4:1-5)
1. Greedy Women of Samaria (4:1-3)
2. Superficial Formalism in Worship (4:4-5)

II. SUFFICIENT WARNING (4:6-11)
1. Lack of Bread (4:6)
2. Shortage of Water (4:7-8)
3. Failure of Crops (4:9)
4. Suffering by Disease and Death (4:10)
5. Overthrow of Cities (4:11)

III. UNMISTAKABLE PUNISHMENT (4:12-13)
1. The Certainty of God's Punishment (4:12)
2. The Adequacy of God's Power (4:13)

5

Inevitable Judgment

AMOS 4

Is THERE ANY vital relationship between Sunday's worship and Monday's pattern of living? Is there justification for expecting some connection between the two? Should worship actually produce tangible effect upon the daily life of a person? The thoughtful Christian will answer each of these questions affirmatively. However, when specific illustrations are sought, the relationships usually become theoretical. Real life situations often raise serious question about the validity of the average churchgoer's worship experience.

I. UNLIMITED CORRUPTION (4:1-5)

Amos considered it an important part of his prophetic task to bring religion to bear upon life. He was not willing to offer an either/or arrangement but demanded a both/and relationship. Amos was constantly aware of a linkage between the daily life of Israel and the working out of God's overall purposes. In like manner, the prophet did not view everyday corruption and oppression as unrelated to the worship system of his day. This type of meaningful connection led Amos to point out two seemingly divergent, but actually interacting, evils.

1. Greedy Women of Samaria (4:1-3)

In one of the most bitter attacks by any prophet upon a particular segment of Israel's society, Amos singled out the wealthy women of Samaria. He addressed them as "cows of Bashan" (v. 1, RSV), in order to describe their pattern of living as purely animal. Their only thought was for their own contentment through food and pleasure. They cared not for the hurt of the less fortunate. Actually, their oppression of the poor and their crushing of the needy was indirect. By saying to their husbands, "Bring, and let us drink," the women were driving their men to oppress the poor increasingly so as to satisfy their animal appetites. Although Amos upbraided them without mercy, he must have recognized how much to be pitied were these thoughtless matrons of Samaria's social register.

The condemnation of the wealthy women involved more than a promise of punishment or denunciation. Amos pictured God as taking an oath toward the fulfilment of this aspect of his purpose. Three times (4:2; 6:8; 8:7) such an oath was recorded by Amos, but only in 4:2 was it based upon God's holiness. The prophet was emphasizing that God had bound himself by his own moral character to act in behalf of the oppressed.

The form of punishment was as shocking as the description of the first ladies of Samaria. When the days of fulfilment arrived, the women would no longer know the contentment of fat cattle grazing on the fertile plains of Bashan, east of the Sea of Galilee. Instead, they would be stripped of their finery and led captive with hooks. Two types of hooks were mentioned: the one used in the nose and lips of unruly cattle and the one used for catching fish (v. 2). It may be that Amos used the two in parallel construction to describe the same process, or he may have added the figure of the fish dangling on a hook to picture the utter helplessness of these women. Whatever the case, hooks were actually used by the Assyrian conquerers only a few years later.

In graphic terms, Amos depicted the women being forced to leave the city through broken places in the wall and following each other in a long train of captives. The column of women, linked by hooks and ropes, would resemble a herd of cows making their way through a gap in a broken fence. Their ultimate destination, called Harmon (v. 3, RSV), remains obscure. Such a place cannot be identified.

The intensity of Amos' feelings and the harshness of his words may obscure the valid application of the message. How little has the basic structure of social life changed since the prophet of Tekoa voiced these words. The demands for luxurious surroundings, expensive food and drink, and satisfaction through pleasure overshadow thoughts for the less fortunate. The drives toward prestige and greater wealth greatly intensify the temptation to press for more and more.

R. L. Honeycutt has used the imagery of Amos to describe similar conditions which still prevail, as he says:

> Not only on the mountains of Samaria, but in the valleys of every community the fat cows of Bashan still feed and fatten themselves. They still hook and gore, push and shove, all the while saying, "Bring us more." Nothing is more corrupt than a society insensitive to the needs of its poor and needy.[1]

2. Superficial Formalism in Worship (4:4-5)

The intensity of Amos' words continued as he shifted from the harsh figure of cattle to the use of irony and sarcasm. He next addressed the people at large concerning the meaningless nature of their worship. The usual call by the religious reformer would be, "Come to Bethel and worship." However, Amos viewed their assembly at the shrines as a time of transgression—literally "rebellion"—against God. He used the same word which he had used repeatedly in the formula, "For three transgressions . . . and for four." The very institutions which should have brought honor to God were viewed as rebellion against him.

Certainly the indictment by Amos was colored by his dislike of the many religious practices taken over from the Canaanites. The process of compromise with the inhabitants of the land and accommodation to their patterns of worship had diluted the demands of Israel's covenant faith. Yet Amos seems to have been more concerned about motive and attitude than about form. He could see that their whole attitude toward God was wrong. The people would offer the required sacrifices in a perfunctory way and make a singsong of the ritual, all the time identifying God with their selfish interests and pleasures. In subordinating God to their own desires, they had developed a smug complacency about life.

It was concerning such a vacuum that Amos spoke. Bethel and Gilgal were both prominent sanctuaries frequented by great throngs of Israelites. Connected with the shrines were pilgrimages which appealed to peoples from widely scattered areas. To these would-be worshipers, Amos directed his sarcastic invitation. After inviting them to come and transgress, he specified four ways to multiply their rebellions.

The reference to bringing of sacrifices every morning and tithes every three days appears to be further sarcastic suggestion of excessive compliance with outward forms of worship. However, Amos may be referring to a normal procedure during a pilgrimage—arriving one day, bringing sacrifice the next morning, and depositing the tithe on the third day. The prophet was further concerned about the offering of leavened cakes, not because of ritual legislation but because of the Israelites' mistaken zeal in trying to make their thanksgiving offerings more savory. Finally, he specified the proclaiming and publishing of freewill offerings as another way of compounding their rebellion. This involved an ostentatious announcement of one's intention, coupled with an invitation to an accompanying feast. How this resembles the behavior of the rich men of Jesus' day who were so roundly condemned by the Master! (See Matt. 6:2; 23:5.)

Amos did not leave a doubt as to the basic motive involved in such a pattern of worship. He reminded his listeners, "For so you love to do, O people of Israel" (Amos 4:5, RSV). Their purpose was not for the glory of God, the praise of his name, the remembrance of his mighty acts, the desire for forgiveness, or thanksgiving for his benefits. In all of their superficial formalism, the motive was the satisfaction of their own desires. In their love of ritual and sacrifice they had exalted their self-centered interests and had, thereby, obscured their vision of God himself.

In spite of the work of Amos and his successors, Israel never learned this vital lesson. Jesus struggled against an even more institutionalized form of religious life in his day. Likewise, the church of today has lost much of the spontaneity which characterized the band of Jesus' disciples and the primitive church. How little of the original "holy contagion" has survived the complex institutions which make up Christendom! Amos would remind us of the keystone of all religious faith—a vital covenant relationship with God. This we know must come through our relationship with Christ and with his people.

II. SUFFICIENT WARNING (4:6–11)

Amos used five calamities as illustrative of events which should have turned Israel back to God. Although the handwriting on the wall was clear to the prophet, no message was seen by the people. The tragic refrain kept coming back, "Yet have ye not returned unto me, saith the Lord" (4:6, 8, 9, 10, 11).

1. *Lack of Bread* (4:6)

The prospect of famine was a constant threat to those of ancient times, even as it is today to the underdeveloped and overpopulated nations. Every person in Amos' audience had heard stories concerning times of famine or had personally experienced the reality of such a calamity. However, Amos was doing more than reminding them of recurring danger. By the use of emphatic pronouns, he was asserting that God was the author of each disaster. God was quoted as saying, "*I on my part* or *I even I* have given you cleanness of teeth," (4:6, author's translation). In the original language, no one could miss the strong emphasis upon God as the causative force.

Since bread was the main sustaining item of diet, literally the staff of life, this event was a dreaded occurrence which should have caused the people to think. In the picturesque phrase, "cleanness of teeth," Amos was describing a condition where there was no food available to cling to the teeth.

Yet, even with such widespread and extreme havoc, the people had not returned to God. Amos was saying, Here was a signpost along the way that you missed.

2. Shortage of Water (4:7-8)

Drought was the frequent companion of famine and usually an important factor in the process. Amos, however, listed it separately as another evident warning to the people of God. He pointed out that the timing of the event at the worst possible moment in the agricultural year increased its catastrophic effect. Normally, the strong winter rains lasted until the end of February and were followed by gentle showers during March and April. In the case at hand, the withholding of the late winter rains stunted the growth of the crops at their most important growing period.

Even more important for Amos' illustration was the local nature of the drought. He doubly emphasized that the rain fell on certain areas but passed by other sections. Likewise, he used verb forms which implied that this happened repeatedly. The populace of the affected areas journeyed from city to city without satisfaction of their needs. Both the timing and the local character of the events suggested strongly that God was at work. Yet, there was no response.

3. Failure of Crops (4:9)

Three different damages to vegetation were mentioned by Amos to describe an occasion of utter devastation. First, the crops were hit by blight, undoubtedly caused by the hot east wind blowing in from the desert. Such a wind brought intense heat which dried out everything in its path. Driving particles of sand would blacken the sky and damage all forms of vegetation. In the second place, the crops were damaged by occasional warm damp rains during the winter, causing the ears of grain to mildew before ripening. A third damage came from the dreadful destructive work of locusts which devoured what remained. The prophet Joel described in detail the devastating effect of locust plagues (Joel 1:4, 12).

Any one of the calamities mentioned would be enough to dishearten the Israelite farmer. The combined effect would be disastrous beyond words. Yet, the reaction of Israel was merely despair without any semblance of returning to God.

4. Suffering by Disease and Death (4:10)

Amos turned next to the warnings which had come to Israel in the form of epidemics. He apparently envisioned a war camp, where pestilence and epidemics were almost the rule rather than the exception. The problems of sanitation were always greater within the unsettled conditions of temporary camp life. The prophet clearly pointed out the severity of the disease attacks by comparing them with the plagues which originated in Egypt and by referring to the odor of the camp. The death rate was so great that burial was much delayed. Those most affected were the "choice young men" of military age who were vastly important to the safety and well-being of the nation. The reference to the sword as a further instrument of death may be figuratively applied to the plagues, or it may relate to the devastating wars which had preceded the peaceful days of Jeroboam II.

The magnitude of the suffering and death here recounted should have brought the people of God to their knees. Amos could not understand how such events could take their toll without some deep reaction within Israel. Yet, no evidence of genuine repentance was forthcoming.

5. Overthrow of Cities (4:11)

Reserved for last is the most destructive of all the visitations attributed to God by Amos. The word which is translated "overthrown" is used frequently of the sudden destruction of Sodom. (See Gen. 19:25, 29; Deut. 29:23; Isa. 13:19; Jer. 49:18.) Seemingly, the prophet had in mind the sudden devastation of an earthquake, one of the most mysterious experiences confronted by ancient man. Nothing could be done to guard against such a catastrophe, and little could be done to escape. There is probably a relation between this event and the earthquake mentioned in the opening verse of the book of Amos. The phrase, "a firebrand plucked out of the burning" was, and still is, a proverbial statement for the experience of being rescued at the last moment.

The use of this event as a climax in the list of warnings was surely an intentional design on the part of Amos to end with a thoroughly unexplainable event. The rumble of earth and buildings alike was more startling than the war machines of an invading enemy. Its instantaneous shock and sudden demolition of property should have caused immediate response and lasting reflection. Yet, Israel failed to be moved to penitence, even in such a dark hour as here described.

The question must be asked and frankly faced: Was Amos justified in attributing each of these events to the hand of God in dealing with his people? The ancient world always believed that natural calamities came as a result of divine anger. The prophets spoke with one voice concerning the provoking of God's anger by wrongdoing. They often recognized the redemptive quality within God's punishment. Since the early Hebrew had little or no idea of what we call "secondary causes," all that happened was directly attributed to God. He was recognized as the Lord of nature and history, declaring himself in life and death, blessing and curse, good and calamity. This belief was a vital part of their concept of God's sovereignty. Amos could not, and would not, separate God's control from that which he had created. However, it must be noted that Amos was more concerned with man's response than with arguing the nature of God's personal acts.

The question of God's relation to suffering is still very much a problem for modern man. In light of the totality of God's revelation in the Bible and in Christ, one cannot attribute all suffering to direct punishment from God. Many are the causes and forces which interact to affect the innocent as well as the guilty. The primary interest of Amos must still be our genuine concern. How do we react and respond to the disasters which befall us? Uncertainty as to their relationship to the purpose of God should lead us to deep reflection and greater desire to understand.

Through catastrophe we should learn that nature does not exist to satisfy our every whim. Suffering is often disciplinary in nature. Through suffering the way for deeper communion with God should be opened as we realize our own dependence upon God. The clearer we see our own frailty and helplessness, the more we sense the greatness and sovereignty of God. Even though we may not be able to indicate precisely which events in life are punishments from God, it would be an extremely hard task to prove that any certain event is not related to his purpose.

III. UNMISTAKABLE PUNISHMENT (4:12-13)

Since God's discipline of his people of Israel had passed unheeded, nothing remained except the declaration of the sentence upon them. The nation had been given sufficient warning, but she would not respond. The people had closed their ears to the voice of God and their eyes to the events designed as discipline to call them back to God.

1. The Certainty of God's Punishment (4:12)

It is surprising to see how Amos worked up to such a climax and then left the punishment unnamed. The statement, "Thus will I do unto thee, O Israel," appears to be an anticlimax when compared with the previous vigorous declarations by the prophet. Although it is possible that part of the text has been lost in the process of transmission, it is more likely that Amos was using this sense of vagueness as a strong literary device. The people would expect a powerful denunciation involving highly descriptive language from the outspoken Amos. Instead, he left the hearers, their imaginations intensified by the graphic descriptions just recounted, free to picture their own deserved punishment. He could have predicted events even more dreadful than any of the preceding visitations. However, such predictions might have been as unheeded as the previous warnings.

This same vague but terrifying feeling is evident in the warning, "Prepare to meet thy God." Amos was not offering the people a method of escape. The judgment of God had already been decreed, although the details had been deliberately omitted. It should be noted that the prophet led the people to the point where they were face to face with God, not with the threatening Assyrian armies or the forces of natural calamity. God was the source and author of their doom. Toward him they must turn. They were accountable to God for their sin and their refusal to heed his evident warnings.

The words of Amos, "Prepare to meet thy God," are often seen on rocks or signs beside the road. There is desperate need today, not for more signs beside the roads, but for voices of authority who will translate this principle into the language of life. The fact that men and nations must meet God in judgment makes imperative a sense of preparation which must invariably involve repentance. As in Amos' day, the object of that preparation is God. While man may prepare for many important events in life, the ultimate and most important readiness relates to man's encounter with God.

2. *The Adequacy of God's Power* (4:13)

The call by Amos to "prepare" naturally involved some explanation of the nature of God, the object of the preparation. In language that reminds us of a hymn, he pointed to the one they had largely forgotten. It is interesting to note the close connection between this doxology and two others in 5:8–9; 9:5–6. John D. W. Watts has presented a strong argument for concluding that these three doxologies were originally an old hymn. He writes: "Amos may well have spoken the words and yet have been quoting familiar fragments of a current hymn." Especially is this idea reasonable in the verse under consideration, since the words fit so well into the context.

The God whom Israel must face was described by Amos as thoroughly equal to the task of judgment and punishment.

As Creator, God was maker of the visible mountains and the invisible wind. These two different forms of matter were often referred to as examples of wonder for the Hebrews. The solid and massive mountains as well as the strange and destructive force of the wind spoke of creative power. Reference to God's act of declaring his thoughts to men reminds one of Amos' previous words concerning God's revelation of his secret counsel to his servants, the prophets (3:8). The agent of revelation here (4:13) may be his prophet, or it may be the inner conscience of man through which the Spirit of God moves. The emphasis is upon God's power to work in the lives of those whom he has created.

The sudden blackening of the sky, as morning is turned into darkness, also demonstrates God's power over the world which he has created. God's treading upon the high places may well be a figure of speech linking God with the thunderstorm, or relating him to the mysterious power of an earthquake. (See Psalm 29.) Without technical knowledge of geology, the ancients often thought of earthquakes as being produced by giant divine steps.

Lest there be some doubt in the minds of his hearers, Amos spelled out the name of the God the people were about to face: Yahweh, the God of the covenant who is also "God of hosts." Such a designation should have reminded the people of their long-ignored covenant responsibilities as well as of God's majesty and omnipotence. In fact, much more was implied for the original hearer or reader, since a name was considered to be descriptive of one's very character. There could be no doubt that God had both the right and the power to accomplish his purpose in judgment.

In a world so egoistic in describing the power of men and nations, the message of God's omnipotence is sorely needed. The ever-increasing self-sufficiency, growing out of an affluent society and worldwide prestige, tends to minimize this message of Amos. The sharp distinction between human and divine power, once clearly realized, has been dimmed by the mushrooming clouds of atomic explosions. The immense steps toward the conquest of space have seemingly closed the gap further. However, while Amos had to describe God's power in terms of the nonscientific knowledge of his day, we have knowledge and language to keep pace with the modern age. God's power has not changed in quantity or quality, but our ability to comprehend and appreciate it has grown. The gap has not been closed between the power of God and the power of man. Instead, the new capabilities of man should heighten our understanding of the omnipotence which brought all things into being. How much more twentieth-century men should stand in awe before God's unlimited power and in dread before his judgment!

FOR CLASS PREPARATION

1. Consider carefully the drives in life for prestige and position in the light of Amos' words (4:1–3). Analyze the way these drives affect your concern and compassion for others.
2. Examine the teachings of Jesus concerning religious leaders to find his reaction to the superficial observances of his day. (See Matt. 6:1–8; 12:1–4; 23:1–36; Luke 11:37–54.)
3. Use a Bible dictionary to find the significance of the names "Yahweh" (Jehovah) and "God of hosts." Note the importance of Hebrew names as designating the character of the one to whom reference is made.

FOR ADVANCED STUDY

1. For further application of Amos' charge of superficial formalism to modern church life:
   R. L. Honeycutt, *Amos and His Message*, pp. 84–85.
2. For a description of the sirocco (hot east wind):
   G. A. Smith, *Geography of the Holy Land*, pp. 67–69.
3. For a discussion of earthquakes in Palestine:
   S. R. Driver, *Joel and Amos* (Cambridge Bible), pp. 171–172.
   L. E. Toombs, "Earthquake," *The Interpreter's Dictionary of the Bible*, E–J, 4.
4. For a concise summary of arguments relating to the date of the doxologies (4:13; 5:8–9; 9:5–6):
   E. A. Edghill, *The Book of Amos*, pp. 46–47.

---

[1] R. L. Honeycutt, *Amos and His Message* (Nashville: Broadman Press, 1963), p. 80.

CHAPTER 6

LAMENTATION FOR A DEAD NATION—AMOS 5

6

Lamentation for a Dead Nation

AMOS 5

HISTORIANS HAVE OFTEN experienced difficulty in determining at what point great powers of the past actually lost the vitality which made them great. The death pangs are often visible for a long period before a nation ceases to be or before a people become swallowed up by aggressive neighbors. The factors which lead to the downfall are usually clearly evident, and the year of defeat is almost always known. However, the exact moment when the spark of greatness disappears and the flame of fortune goes out is much harder to detect.

For Amos there was no doubt about the immediate future for Israel. She had lost the spark which had made her great. She had allowed the eternal flame of the covenant to flicker and be extinguished. Although the armies of Assyria had not begun their triumphant march, Israel was as good as dead!

1. OBITUARY FOR ISRAEL (5:1-3)

Amos again varied his method of presentation, showing unusual skill in communicating his message. He announced his approach by using a lamentation or dirge. This was a type of funeral song used in ancient Israel, usually chanted by women who acted as professional mourners. Rather than an uncontrolled and spontaneous utterance, the dirge was a planned composition based upon a definite poetical form. S. R. Driver has well described its peculiar rhythm and strange effect, saying:

> As a rule, in Hebrew poetry, the second of two parallel members balances the first, being approximately similar in length and structure, and presenting a thought either synony-

72

mous with it, or antithetic to it; but in the Hebrew elegy, the second member is shorter than the first, and instead of balancing and re-enforcing it, echoes it imperfectly, producing a plaintive, melancholy cadence.[1]

This pattern of rhythm, three beats followed by two, continues with all its pathos through Amos 5 : 2–6 and dominates much of the entire chapter. By such a method Amos was communicating with sound as well as word. It may be that he used some visual means of supporting and augmenting his truth. The prophet Ezekiel used all manner of pantomimes to illustrate his message. The nature of Amos' words would suggest that he may have appeared dressed as a mourner with torn garments and ashes upon his head. Such a costume would have immediately identified the prophet with the main thrust of his tidings.

1. The Fallen Virgin (5:2)

When seen in poetic form, the opening words which Amos used are striking indeed.

> Fallen, no more to rise,
> is the virgin Israel;
> forsaken on her land,
> with none to raise her up.
> —RSV

While the actual rhythm of the original cannot be produced in English translation, the plaintive nature of word and sound is evident. Amos chose to use verbs which presented the event as an already accomplished fact. He did not date the time of death, but he knew that there was no doubt about the certainty of it. Although the nation was able to linger at least thirty years politically, she had already sold her birthright to life.

The figure of Israel as a virgin was seemingly new in Amos' day. Amos used this figure of speech to speak of Israel as previously undefiled by complete foreign domination. The scene envisioned was that of a young maiden lying on the ground, despoiled by the conquerer. She had been abandoned and forsaken without any possibility of help. The great tragedy lay in the fact that she was still in the bloom of life with her ambitions and purposes yet unrealized. Such an untimely end for one so young and so full of promise should break the hardest heart. Yet, this was not really a young maiden about which Amos was talking; it was a nation at the height of her prosperity and secure in her military successes. How could this peasant from the wilderness be so sure of what he prophesied?

2. *The Tenth Part Remaining* (5:3)

Amos punctuated his dramatic illustration with the badge of his credentials: "For thus saith the Lord God." Upon the authority of God, the prophet defined the odds for the proud people of Israel. There was the hope of a remnant surviving, but how pitifully small in comparison to the ever-growing population. The loss of nine out of ten from the ranks of the army would quickly reduce the nation to the level of complete servitude. Such losses were viewed as accomplished for large cities and small villages. One doom was common to all; the city could not rely upon its strength nor the village upon its obscurity.

II. TRUE AND FALSE RELIGION (5:4-6)

The Israelites of Amos' day practiced religion with a zeal perhaps exceeding that of any previous period in their history. The conditions of prosperity and peace made possible more leisure time, more resources for gifts and sacrifices, and less distraction from harassment by enemies. Why then was Amos so intent upon sweeping away the national shrines and sanctuaries? Not because of inactivity or lack of interest! Not simply because of taints of idolatry which had crept in! Amos continually condemned the entire system of worship, tithes, sacrifice, and ritual. He considered all religious ceremony, as practiced by Israel, an abomination to the Lord. He could see that the ritual ceremonies had become ends in themselves, obliterating "the weightier matters of the law" and obscuring the very God the people pretended to worship. Stress upon the ceremonial was the distinguishing characteristic of paganism. This same attitude had permeated the religion of Israel so as to make ritual a mechanical atonement unrelated to life and a substitute for true morality. For Amos, the only hope lay in sweeping away the ceremonial so that a spiritual foundation based on moral principles could be built.

1. The Command to Seek God (5:4)

While Amos regarded ritual expressions of religion as dispensable, he would quickly affirm that there were matters which were thoroughly indispensable. At the top of the list stood a sincere seeking after God—not after some means toward God, but God himself. How wonderfully concise were the two words in Amos' language: "Seek . . . and . . . live"! The use of two successive imperatives made this commandment as emphatic as it was concise.

The word translated "seek" originally referred to the obtaining of a decision or an answer to a question from a seer, a prophet, or a priest. The one so seeking was thus desiring a divine solution to a problem. However, the word changed direction in meaning, or at least in agency, pointing toward a longing for God in a much deeper sense. Seeking after God came to stand for that Godward direction of life by which one sought his will and lived life accordingly.

A similar seeking after God was specified in Deuteronomy 4:29. There it is promised that the Lord shall be found "if thou seek him with all thy heart and with all thy soul." It was this type of search which Amos had in mind rather than the desire to placate an angry god or gain some favor—factors normally motivating the ancient worshiper. Man can find life only when he seeks God with all his being and finds him as the meaning for all his life.

2. The Demand to Refuse Substitutes (5:5-6)

The Israelites had never realized that going to a place where religious people gather is not the same as "seeking

God." Going to a sanctuary is relatively easy; meeting God and finding genuine motivation for life is quite another thing. The spiritual nature of God makes worship a thing of the spirit rather than simply a matter of place. (See John 4:24.) The Israelites have their modern counterparts.

In verse 5 Amos indulged in an effective play of words, using the verb translated "seek" again in a different sense and employing words which sound or look somewhat alike. Three places were singled out as possible substitutes for the true worship of God. The first two, Bethel and Gilgal, were major sanctuaries in the Northern Kingdom of Israel. The third, Beersheba, lay in the extreme south of Judah, about fifty miles to the south-southeast of Jerusalem. This was a shrine associated originally with the patriarchs. Seemingly the people of Israel passed over the border and made pilgrimages to the sanctuary there.

Previously, Amos had sarcastically said, "Come to Bethel, and transgress; at Gilgal multiply transgression" (4:4). Here he straightforwardly demanded that they have nothing to do with these substitutes. The people in record numbers were superficially seeking God. However, the shrines and sanctuaries had become an opiate of the masses, replacing the vital relationship between God and his people. Amos could sense that the traditions and rituals of the past had degenerated into a cheap form of substitution for heartfelt religion. He knew that the end was close for both Bethel and Gilgal. Beersheba was not named for destruction, since it lay outside the boundaries of Israel and was thus only indirectly related to the problem at hand.

The admonition by God in 5:4 was repeated again in verse 6 to impress further the cardinal principle upon which man responds to God. This time a fresh motive in the form of a threat was given for seeking God. There is serious question whether another chance to escape punishment and captivity was being offered to Israel. The dirge which opened the chapter had such a finality about it as to preclude any hope for a second chance at this late date. The whole message of Amos was pointed toward an inevitable doom. However, several outstanding scholars see that there was a ray of hope that destruction might be averted if Israel would seek the Lord and live (5:6) as well as seek good and live (v. 14).

This plea would certainly be in harmony with the character of God as recognized by Amos. Yet, even if the possibility were there, the people's unresponsiveness made it entirely theoretical. Amos closed the chapter with further reference to the exile. His task as prophet was to prepare the people for the certainty of doom.

Time has not changed the importance of Amos' admonition to seek God and live. A greater prophet than Amos, Christ Jesus, reinterpreted this truth for all men, saying: "Seek ye first the kingdom of God, and his righteousness" (Matt. 6:33). In answer to the perennial question for every age, How must we seek God? he said: "I am the way, the truth, and the life: no man cometh unto the Father, but by me . . . he that hath seen me hath seen the Father" (John 14:6–9). Not only did Christ give direction to the process of seeking God, he pointed all who would receive to the abundant life which comes as an integral part of finding God.

Modern man needs desperately to discover that traditional patterns of worship can never be an adequate substitute for a personal relationship with God gained from truly seeking after him and his will. Even though the way to the Father through Christ is marvelously clear, this way can be obscured when something other than involvement with God is given first place. Traditional approaches, whether of ritual or methods, can finally gain the status of a mechanical atonement for obvious shortcomings in daily life.

There is no firmer foundation for abundant life than the genuine seeking (and finding) of God through Christ. Symbol, ritual, ceremony, and methodology all have a place within the Christian life; but they must be dispensable when they tend to eclipse the goal of seeking God "with all thy heart and with all thy soul" (Deut. 4:29).

III. Social Justice (5:7-17)

Amos was not shifting from the realm of the religious to the sphere of the secular at this point in his message. He regarded all life as governed by the righteous will of a righteous God. His fellowmen might class offenses in daily life as unrelated to their duties at the sanctuary. Not so with the prophet from Tekoa! He believed that how a man responded to another in the marketplace was a barometer of his own insight and knowledge about God. Amos' whole concept of social justice was an outgrowth of his understanding of the righteous character of God. Such a consciousness had come from the prophet's own pilgrimage in seeking and finding all of life in God.

1. *The Bitterness of Injustice* (5:7-9)

The administration of judgment should involve hope for the innocent, the downtrodden, and the afflicted. The very justification for courts of law has always been that in some way vindication could be accomplished. Amos could see plainly that the whole process of law had been reversed in Israel. Instead of being the hope of the hopeless, judgment had been turned to bitterness (wormwood). In the Old Testament, the wormwood plant represented that which was bitter, repugnant, and hateful. The rights of the common persons had been denied them, bringing bitterness and hate instead of justice. In parallel form, Amos spoke of righteousness as being cast down or left off instead of occupying its proper place in the affairs of God's covenant people.

How long is the trail of bitterness coming out from repudiated justice and righteousness! The conflict between Cain and Abel was but a foretaste of man's inhumanity to man. The struggle has continued between farmer and shepherd, rural and urban groups, rich and poor, powerful and weak, as well as minority and majority divisions of society. Too often property rights have been the primary consideration rather than personal rights. The story of Ahab's injustice in demanding and taking the vineyard of Naboth illustrates well the deep bitterness which results from the rejection of human rights. (See 1 Kings 21.)

The message of Amos on social justice is broken by the second doxology (5:8–9) describing the power and majesty of God. The section would more logically follow verse 6, since verse 7 introduces the discussion continued in verse 10. The King James Version seeks to solve the problem by adding the words "seek him" as an introduction to the doxology. However, the break is not without purpose in that it reminds the reader of the nature of the One who should be sought rather than defied.

God is again pictured as the all-powerful Creator and the ruler of heaven and earth. The constellations, Pleiades and Orion, are often mentioned by the ancients because of their relative brilliance and their relationship to the seasons. (See Job 9:9; 38:31.) Amos' object in this passage is to show that God cannot be limited in his concern for all men nor localized within the confines of a sanctuary. It is God who has placed the stars in orbit, who ushers in each day, who turns day into night, and who brings the refreshing rains to his creation. Likewise it is God who confounds the imagined strength of proud men and cities.

Such a concept of God transcends the limitations of time and space. Not only did God bring all things into being by his creation, he continues to sustain that which he made. His relationship is not alone to natural phenomena but also to the historical affairs in the life of man. Amos was trying to lead Israel out of the trap which she had built, in which God was supposedly localized in a certain sanctuary or limited to a particular traditional pattern. The prophet was pointing in a general way toward the truth which Jesus later emphasized in John 4:23.

2. *The Brutal Treatment of the Poor* (5:10–13)

The conduct of the merchants and leading citizens of Israel went beyond the bounds of "good business." Amos could see no justification for the brutality and thoughtlessness of those who knew better. No society, ancient or modern, could rationalize the practices described, although many nations have been equally guilty. However, seldom has there been a prophet such as Amos to point out the brutality with similar effectiveness.

(1) *The setting.*—The references to the "gate" bring up an important aspect of Israel's life (5:10, 12, 15). The usual place for the administration of justice was the area within the opening in the city wall where the main gate was located. The size of the accommodations depended upon the thickness of the wall system. Seats in the form of stone benches probably lined either side. Here the "elders" would sit as a popular council or forum. (See Gen. 23:10; 34:20; Deut. 25:7; Ruth 3:11; 4:1, 11; Job 31:21; Psalm 127:5.)

(2) *The charges.*—Amos set forth a series of indictments which seem to apply most specifically to the elders or judges who arbitrated in the gate. Certainly much of the blame and judgment applied to the wealthy members of society who were in a position to influence the decisions of the council for their own benefit. These persons in places of responsibility were heedless to the cries of the less fortunate. They expressed hate for the one who exposed sinful injustice and abhorred the honesty of those who were innocent of the charges (5:10). They took advantage of the weakness of the poor by trampling upon their rights and exacting either penalties or enforced gifts of wheat from them (5:11). These leaders did not fool God, since he knew how they inflicted deep hurt upon both the just ones and the needy (5:12). The word translated "bribe" more properly denoted a ransom paid for the pardon of a murderer. While the rich could literally get away with murder, the poor but just ones had no chance.

(3) *The penalty.*—Although there was seldom justice "in the gate," Amos was able to point toward retribution for those dispensing injustice. They were using their ill-gotten gains to build the ultimate in fine homes—those constructed of stones carefully shaped by the hands of underpaid and oppressed workmen (v. 11). They were further planting

vineyards, expecting to reap the harvest for years to come. Amos promised that they would not have opportunity to enjoy either, since God's judgment was at hand.

The admonition in verse 13 to keep silent is difficult to reconcile with the life and purpose of the outspoken prophet from Tekoa. In fact, it stands in direct opposition to all which he represented. Some commentators regard this statement as looking forward to the time of God's punishment. Others treat it as a later addition to his message. Still other writers would suggest that Amos was only quoting a common proverb of his day. If it is applied to the days of Amos, it must express the utter hopelessness of the situation at the moment and for the visible future. Certainly Amos never applied such a proverb to his own right to speak.

3. The Connection Between Religion and Morality (5:14-17)

The basic cause of the blindness to injustice by Israel's leaders lay in their conscious or unconscious divorcing of morality from religion. While the religion of Israel was more concerned with morality than that of other nations, the people in Amos' day did not demonstrate this concern in actual practice. They imagined that God would graciously overlook their acts of oppression as long as they carried out their ritual responsibilities at the sanctuary.

Amos turned dramatically from negative condemnation to positive admonition, using a series of imperatives to awaken Israel's dormant, moral conscience. The command to "seek good" must be understood in terms of the previous injunction to "seek God" (5:4, 6). In each case, the corollary was life in its fullest and most meaningful aspects. While Amos was linking good (in the sense of moral values) with God, he carefully avoided the temptation of many moralists to substitute morality for God.

By first directing the people toward God as the object of life's meaning, the prophet laid a foundation upon which God could be known as the basis of all morality. It was because of God's essentially moral character that he had a right to demand moral behavior of Israel. Amos affirmed that their only hope of having God with them resided in the moral goodness of their lives. Only in hating evil, loving good, and establishing justice in the gate could they be sure of a gracious response by God.

Amos (vv. 16–17) reverted to the dark picture of mourning with which the chapter began. The lament for a dead nation was described as reaching out into the streets, highways, and vineyards. Those not usually involved in funeral lamentations would soon join the professional mourners, all sharing in a common wailing refrain. While the dirge (cf. 5:1–3) was the province of the professionals, all could join in the common cries of lamentation such as "Alas, alas." This vivid description of universal mourning demonstrated that Amos was not expecting any reprieve for Israel. All that the prophet could hope for was spiritual orientation for a remnant who would survive. It was on this basis that Amos could continue to warn and exhort people.

In a day when strange concepts of morality are gaining favor among many Christian leaders, the message of Amos is especially relevant. Much within the "new morality" is as old as, and as insidious as, the pagan concepts of the ancient Canaanites. The tendency is to separate morality from the realm of revealed religion, making God and good entirely separate objects of man's seeking. Such perversions, whether ancient or modern, can lead only toward destruction. If Amos were present today, is there any doubt that he would already hear the haunt of wailing refrains? How much America needs a prophetic voice capable of reaching both leaders and masses with the call to "seek God, hate evil, love good, and establish justice" in our land!

IV. The Coming Day (5:18–25)

Amos was certain that the status quo could not be maintained. Israel had sown her wild oats without regard to the cries of humanity. The prophet was convicted that a coming day would bring a violent change in Israel.

1. *The Day of Darkness* (5:18–20)

There was a popular view current in Israel that the Day of the Lord would be a day of victory for God's people and a day of disaster for all enemies. This view presented a Utopian situation whereby God's action would be ultimate light and brightness for his people. It was natural for such bright hope to be anticipated in the time of peace and prosperity. By the time of Amos, a cliché had probably become common by which any pessimistic outlook could be dismissed by saying, in essence: "Just wait until the Day of the Lord arrives."

For Amos the popular view was hopelessly superficial. He emphasized that whether God would come in judgment or blessing would depend upon Israel's moral condition. The victory of God would be over sin rather than over the political enemies of his chosen people. God's righteousness must be vindicated against both the sin of Israel and the sin of foreign powers.

It should be apparent that Amos did not throw out the basic idea which had arisen as an element of hope; he introduced a moral basis which gave real authority to the concept. In view of Israel's repudiation of morality in life and deed, the "light" must become "darkness." While the enemies of Israel would be punished, Amos maintained that the basis of determining punishment for all nations would be the relation of each to God's demand for righteousness and justice. There would be no escape, since one danger leads to another. For Israel, the bright day was reversed into the darkest of nights.

Are these words of Amos canceled by the light of the gospel of Christ? Are nations now judged by some other measure than the standard of God's righteousness? If the prophet Amos could speak now, he would answer with a resounding *No!* Men still derive false security from an idea of favored status which is devoid of moral responsibility. Just as Israel confused externals with living faith, men today rely upon outer forms without inner moral content. Many persons enthusiastically look for the return of Christ as the panacea of all troubles in life, and speak of the coming of the kingdom of God without adequate regard for God's ethical demands upon his children. Jesus clearly spoke of judgment as a time of darkness and travail (Luke 13:28; Matt. 24:3ff). How closely our smug complacency parallels the people of Israel rather than the teaching of God through Amos and Christ!

2. *The Reform of Worship* (5:21-25)

Amos had previously denounced in general terms the type of ritualism practiced by Israel. Here he became quite specific in stating God's reaction to feast days, ceremonial assemblies, burnt offerings, meal offerings, peace offerings, and even the songs and accompanying instruments. At first glance, it appears that Amos was sweeping away all worship forms in order to present a new system of worship. However, comparison with his previous statements and with the writings of Isaiah, Jeremiah, and Malachi would suggest an altogether different conclusion. The prophetic intent was one of reformation rather than revolution and innovation.

Amos was not ruling out the possible use of the ceremonial, but he was strongly condemning the pattern of ritual and sacrifice *as practiced* by his contemporaries. Amos believed that religion was not dependent on the sacrificial system, for Israel had worshiped without sacrifices in the wilderness. It should be carefully noted that Amos' purpose was purification rather than abolition. However, under the circumstances of his day, the only hope seemed to lie in rejection of the substitutes in order to return to the fundamentals of the faith. New Testament worship has no need of such rituals; indeed, in Christ they have been abolished.

The reference to idols and images in verse 26 presents another side of Israel's perversion of the true faith. While the verse is impossible to translate precisely, the intent of the passage seems clear. The worship system with its absorption of pagan influences would go into captivity along with the heedless Israelites. The location "beyond Damascus" (5:27) clearly points to the rising Assyrian kingdom.

The true alternative for the problem of Israel's superficial ceremonialism lay in letting "justice roll down like waters, and righteousness like an everflowing stream" (5:24, RSV). Nothing else could stem the tide of meaninglessness in religion. Amos was hereby calling for a release of the pent-up justice and righteousness in the lives of the Israelites. The word for "stream" referred to a watercourse which dried up during all but a part of the year. During the rainy season, the water flowed as a torrent in such streams. Amos was attempting to break the dam so the water could be ever-flowing rather than occasional.

John Bright has aptly summed up the application of Amos' message in this chapter, saying:

> The intent of Amos' message, then, is plain—as plain as a blow in the face. Nor is there need to argue that it is a relevant message in all ages; it is desperately relevant. It tells us what we need to hear: that a society that cares more for gain than for honor, for its living standard than for God, is sick to the death; that a church which has no rebuke for society, which demands lavish support before righteous behavior, is no true church but a sham of a church. Amos tells us that no amount of religious activity and loyalty to church can make a man's conduct in business and society of no concern to God, nor can a correct creed play substitute for plain obedience to the divine Will in all aspects of life. He tells us that a church which makes a dichotomy between faith and ethics, to the point of making small insistence upon the latter, is under the judgment of God along with the society of which it has become a part.[2]

FOR CLASS PREPARATION

1. Examine the following passages for understanding of other descriptions of the Day of the Lord by the prophets: Isaiah 13:6–16; Joel 1:15–20; 2:1–11; 3:9–18; Obadiah 15; Zephaniah 1:7–17; 3:9–13; Malachi 4:5–6.
2. Make a list of ceremonial substitutes which may obscure the vital presence of God. Remember that these are not necessarily

bad in essence but may become so if they become ends in themselves.

3. Consider seriously the treatment of the poor and outcast in your own community. Analyze ways in which you and your church can do more in accepting responsibility for social justice.

FOR ADVANCED STUDY

1. For further insight into mourning practices in ancient Israel:
   S. R. Driver, *Joel and Amos* (Cambridge Bible), pp. 232–234.
   Edmond Jacob, "Mourning," *Interpreter's Dictionary of the Bible*, K–Q, 452–454.
2. For a summary of prophetic attitudes toward ritualism:
   J. P. Hyatt, *Prophetic Religion*, pp. 118–132.
3. For a more detailed study of Amos' attitude toward sacrifice:
   R. S. Cripps, *The Book of Amos* (Rev. Ed., 1955), pp. xxviii ff.
4. For an examination of the Day of the Lord in prophetic literature:
   H. W. Robinson, *Inspiration and Revelation*, pp. 135–147.
   J. M. P. Smith, *The Day of Yahweh*.

---

[1] S. R. Driver (ed.), *The Cambridge Bible for Schools and Colleges: The Books of Joel and Amos* (Cambridge: University Press, 1901), XXV, 175.

[2] John Bright, *The Kingdom of God* (New York: Abingdon Press, 1953), pp. 62–63.

CHAPTER 7

THE HARVEST OF SELFISH LUXURY—AMOS 6

I. PRIDE AND SELF-INDULGENCE (6:1–7)
  1. The Leaders at Ease in Zion (6:1–6)
  2. The Same Leaders First into Exile (6:7)

II. SUFFERING AND CAPTIVITY (6:8–14)
  1. The Anguish of Siege (6:8–11)
  2. The Fall of the Proud (6:12–14)

7

The Harvest of Selfish Luxury

AMOS 6

Happiness has been an object of unending search for mankind. The sense of well-being and security has been a desire common to every era, every culture, and every level of society. The idea of material prosperity almost always enters the picture. Happiness is equated with peace and plenty.

However, when prosperity arrives, the dream is seldom, if ever, realized. Many of the old problems remain and are intensified by the inequalities which result. The rich may become richer, the merchants more successful, and the leaders more powerful. But almost invariably the poor fail to share in the increase, making broader the gap between the "haves" and the "have-nots." Too often prosperity results in oppression and injustice rather than happiness. Such was the pattern of life to which Amos addressed himself.

I. Pride and Self-indulgence (6:1-7)

Israel always had a deep sense of pride because of her unique position in the purposes of God. This pride, previously referred to by Amos, had become the special province of those most responsible for the era of peace and prosperity. The rising fortunes of Israel had provided the opportunity for the leaders to express their pride in a reckless type of self-indulgence. They could even justify their actions theologically by claiming that all was well, since God's blessings were evident upon their efforts. However, the keen eyes of Amos were able to pierce the veneer which glossed over their sins. Amos interpreted the same circumstances in quite a different way.

1. The Leaders at Ease in Zion (6:1-6)

Amos recognized a relaxed atmosphere in the affairs on "Capitol Hill" in Samaria. The leading citizens lived a life of contentment and tranquility, oblivious to all that was going on about them. They were so "at ease" as to be insensible to the real dangers surrounding the nation. They were so wrapped up in their newly-acquired luxuries that they could not hear the cries of the masses. Life had become one big party to which only their peers were invited. The basic problem which Amos saw was not that the rich were enjoying life. He spoke out against their "ease" at the expense of those less fortunate ones who were paying for the indulgences of the rich and who would soon suffer even more in captivity. In demonstrating the magnitude of the problem, Amos pointed out three evidences of the condition described as "ease in Zion."

(1) Mistaken security (6:1).—Those who enjoyed the easy life had lulled themselves into a false sense of security, placing their confidence in the hill of Samaria rather than in God. Although there was pride in the defensive capabilities of the excellently placed city, the error mentioned may well refer to a false political confidence. The phrase, "the notable men of the first of the nations" (RSV), was probably used by Amos as an ironical description of the leaders' opinion of themselves and Israel's opinion of herself. The irony seems to continue in regard to the crowds who flocked to Samaria for judgment. The people from all over the kingdom came expecting justice but found a mistaken security among unconcerned nobles.

(2) Negligent thoughtlessness (6:2-3).—Those obsessed with their own importance could not understand what was going on in the outside world or what God was about to do. Amos' reference to the comparison between Israel and the cities, Calneh, Hamath, and Gath is difficult to understand. Amos may be continuing the irony begun in verse 1 or indicating that Israel has been blessed far more than the other nations. Regardless of the reason for the comparison, Amos

placed his emphasis on the manner in which the leaders "put far away the evil day" and caused "the seat of violence to come near" (6:3). By claiming security and ignoring the danger signs of the time, they were dismissing all serious thought. They refused to think about a time of calamity, driving from their minds the approaching "day." They spent their time practicing violence, ignoring justice. Amos was attempting to remind them that no matter how they tried to postpone the day of judgment it was sure to come. No amount of ignoring reality could change the obvious verdict of God.

(3) *Heartless indifference* (6:4–6).—The most graphic picture of the easy life among Samaria's elite concerned the extravagant luxuries which illustrated their heartless indifference to the needs of others. The items mentioned were most likely to incur the wrath of a nomadic shepherd like Amos. However, it must be realized that Amos was reaching below the surface to catalog the indulgences which characterized the life of those blinded to the cries of the oppressed. He was thus doing more than condemning city life as a whole. The indulgences were symptomatic of much deeper ills which were destroying the very soul of Israel. These points of the prophet's condemnation could not be viewed as sin by Old Testament law if entirely separated from the context. Yet, the sum total presented a vivid picture of excessive indulgence and gross indifference.

The easy life was characterized by the extravagant furniture which typified the affluent era. The type of ivory inlays used in construction of beds has been found at several sites in Palestine and Syria. Carvings of figures and animals were applied to both furniture and walls to add greatly to its decorative value (cf. 6:4; 1 Kings 22:39). The practice of stretching out on couches probably related to the eating of banquet-type meals. While this was frequent practice in New Testament times, the system was first mentioned here in the biblical record and may have been a Syrian importation. The idea behind the word translated "stretch" could be better conveyed by the picture of one sprawled or draped across the couch.

The second illustration of affluence concerned the type of food eaten by the idle rich. As previously mentioned, meat was not a part of the daily diet of the Israelites. Only on ceremonial occasions or in connection with special events would their animals be used for food, since milk and wool were vital commodities. Amos pointed not only to the eating of meat but to the extravagant use of the most delicate lambs and calves before they supplied wool or milk.

The practice of singing "idle songs to the sound of the harp" (6:5, RSV) was a third example of living "at ease." Amos was describing the manner of improving songs in an idle way at their banquets. As far as the prophet was concerned, this was a meaningless endeavor designed only to while away the time. Linked with this was the inventing of other instruments for accompaniment of their extemporized songs.

A fourth case in point concerned the drinking habits of the social leaders. They were not content with ordinary cups but demanded large bowls or basins for their wine. Since this word for "bowl" was used exclusively in the Old Testament for vessels used in religious ceremonies, Amos may be decrying the misuse of such sacred vessels. However, the main thrust appears to be toward the inordinate desires of these luxurious nobles.

The final example of the easy life in Samaria related to the use of fine oils for anointing of the body. While the practice was usually mentioned in connection with religious observances, oil may have frequently been used in moderation as an expression of joy and gladness. However, in this context, the use of oil was simply another indication of extravagance at the expense of the poor.

Amos carefully built up toward his climax by contrasting what these leaders *have* been doing with what they *should* have been doing. They indulged in all manner of extravagance, "but they are not grieved for the affliction of Joseph"

(6:6). Amos was implying that these men and women with time on their hands had a responsibility to be concerned about the moral ruin of Israel. It was their job to give serious thought to the needs of Israel's populace and to the judgment about to fall on the nation. How tragic it was that Amos' warnings could not penetrate the indifferent ears of those bent upon their own selfish pleasures!

(4) *Remarkable parallels.*—The words of Amos appear to be so real in relation to contemporary society that they shock the observant Christian. The temptation comes to apply them exactly as stated by Amos 2,700 years ago. Yet, a thinking person must admit that our society when compared with other societies, both past and present, has realistically applied many of the teachings from the prophets and from Christ.

Christian principles, involved in the founding of our nation, undergird the basic rights accorded to all men. Many injustices, common to ancient nations, have been partially or largely corrected. The witness of Christian churches reaches cities, towns, and rural areas as a constant reminder of the responsibilities which God demands in man-to-man dealings. It is not difficult to build a case to support the claim that America is the most progressive and greatest nation ever to occupy this planet. However, was not this attitude the fatal error of Israel in Amos' day? Compared to the pagan nations, the people of God in Israel and Judah stood ten feet tall.

While America has made great strides in dealing with the perplexing problems of social justice, only the hem of the garment has been touched. The principle that privilege brings responsibility, so clearly enunciated by Amos, applies doubly when viewed in the light of Christ's teaching to man. John Bright has said:

> Wherever men who have known of righteousness can speak only of their right to crowd for what they can get; wherever men who have known of Christian brotherhood behave as if they believed in favored races; wherever men who have heard

a higher calling grow soft in the enjoyment of the ease that money can buy—there is a society under judgment.[1]

The basic problems involved in luxury and indifference still exist—some greater and some lesser in intensity. The elegant beds and couches, the meat delicacies, the idle songs, the flagrant use of strong drink, and the anointing of the body with costly cosmetics—all are now in exaggerated use beyond the wildest imagination of Amos. Many of these things cited by Amos are not evil in themselves. However, the inordinate desire for such things is often symptomatic of deeper ills.

For most Americans, seeking after God and his righteousness comes last, after all these things, rather than first. Smug complacency toward the needs of the less fortunate becomes a creeping paralysis which keeps the church from denouncing injustice, greed, immorality, and corruption in government. The "economic index" points to greater prosperity and fuller employment, lulling our nation into a sense of security and well-being. Our churches shrug off the statistics demonstrating lack of interest in things spiritual and lack of concern for the needs of men. Could it possibly be denied that we are "at ease in Zion"? Are we living beyond the day of God's judgment in history, or are we too great to experience God's hammer of judgment?

2. The Same Leaders First into Exile (6:7)

The word "therefore" introduced the inevitable consequences upon those whom Amos called "the notable men of the first of the nations" (6:1, RSV). Their self-indulgence and their indifference to the cries of the needy would assure them a place in the exile to come. In fact, Amos promised that they would retain a place of leadership— heading the long procession of captives. The once proud nobles would be humbled as they passed as captives through one village after another. Amos also referred to the end of the revelry or banqueting by those who had stretched themselves upon the couches.

II. Suffering and Captivity (6:8–14)

Having introduced the idea of exile for the most guilty, Amos continued the thought by describing more specifically the punishment to come upon the nation. Although exile was still the ultimate destination of the people as well as the leaders, there were other aspects of conquest which would precede the end.

1. *The Anguish of Siege* (6:8–11)

The absolute certainty of the impending punishment was again vouched for by reference to an oath taken by God (see 4:2; 8:7). The fact that he had sworn by himself (literally "by his soul") pointed to the authority of his own character as proof of fulfilment. The reason given for such strong language was God's abhorence of "the pride of Jacob," or Israel, (RSV) and his hatred of the objects of Israel's pride, such as her palaces. The phrase, translated "the excellency of Jacob" (KJV), may refer to splendor or majesty but more probably to deep-seated pride which Israel manifested in her attitude toward recent achievements. This was more than a justifiable pride in a job well done. Her mistaken sense of security based upon a unique position, her negligent thoughtlessness as to the certainty of the Day of the Lord, and her heartless indifference to the inequalities of life were clear evidences of this pride. Just as God hated the meaninglessness of Israel's worship, he hated the proud temper of the nation. It was upon this basis that God affirmed that he would deliver up or hand over everything in the proud city of Samaria. That to which Samaria would be delivered is not mentioned in the text. Whether Amos meant "to an enemy" or "to pestilence" is not clear. The verses which follow would suggest that a combination of both ideas may be present.

The context seems to demand a siege by an enemy, followed by the attendant curses of famine and plague. Such a combination of events was commonplace during invasions by enemy forces. The population would shut themselves up securely in the walled city and rely upon limited supplies of water and food. All too often the siege of a city lasted for many months before the walls actually fell. In fact, Samaria was under siege by the Assyrian armies for eighteen months before being conquered. Suffering was not limited to those who perished by sword, arrow, or spear. Fires within the city brought horror to women and children seeking shelter. Poor sanitation and scarcity of water added to sickness and disease, making frequent the epidemics which could wipe out whole families.

Amos described such an epidemic with ghastly realism in verses 9–10. His purpose was both to awaken his hearers and to prepare them for the terrors about to fall. The vividness of the description and the specific nature of the details make this section appear to be the words of an eyewitness who observed one of the plagues of the period prior to Amos' ministry.

The intensity of the plague was shown by the fact that of ten men remaining after the siege, all would die. The episode told of one man still lingering just short of death when the next of kin came to remove the bodies. The reference to the relative as the one "who burns him" may refer to a rare occasion of cremation in biblical times or to the burning of spices in honor of the dead. The warning not to mention "the name of the Lord" accorded with the Old Testament practice of not speaking the actual name of the covenant God. However, the use here seems to relate to a superstitious dread of inciting God to bring further pestilence. S. R. Driver suggests the possibility of a custom whereby a prayer or an invocation would be offered upon the occasion of death. This would certainly explain the strange warning in a context which does not demand such a reference.

The words of verse 11 serve to complete the prophecy of verse 8 that God would deliver up the entire city of Samaria. Both the great house and the small house fall into the same category—destined for destruction. The idiom used by Amos is best translated by the RSV: "The great house shall

be smitten into fragments, and the little house into bits"
(6:11). While the agent of destruction is not mentioned, the
certainty of the event is clearly established; and the severity
of the punishment is quite evident.

2. *The Fall of the Proud* (6:12–14)

Amos continued his analysis of Israel's end with two
questions designed to be preposterous. Surely no one in
Amos' day would argue that horses could run on rocky crags
or that a farmer would plow the sea with oxen. Equally
absurd was the way in which Israel had perverted justice
and righteousness. Instead of something good and helpful,
justice had become poison, and righteousness had become
as the bitterness of wormwood. Surely no one would try to
define justice as poison or righteousness as bitterness. Yet,
these were the operating definitions as far as Israel's practice
of them was concerned.

Although the people were rejoicing in some recent victory over the Syrians (v. 13), Amos could not share their
enthusiasm. Seemingly he was referring to two towns on the
east of the Jordan River, Lo-debar and Karnaim, rather than
speaking of the meaning which these names had (compare
KJV and RSV). The proud attitude of the people was
demonstrated by their claim that the military victories came
from their own strength. In reality, the Syrians were pre-
occupied with the threatening force of the Assyrians.

According to the well-known axiom in Proverbs 16:18,
"Pride goeth before destruction," Israel had an adequate
supply of the first ingredient; the second was not far away.
Time was running out fast when Amos reminded the people that God had said, "I will raise up against you a nation"
(6:14). This reference was vague in that the nation was not
named, but it was specific in that it was "a nation" whom
God had chosen as the instrument of his punishment. Thus
the geographical extent of the oppression was described in
terms of the account of Jeroboam's conquests: "He restored
the border of Israel from the entrance of Hamath as far as
the Sea of the Arabah" (2 Kings 14:25, RSV). The entrance

to Hamath was the frontier pass leading from the northern border of Israel between the Lebanon ranges toward Hamath, some 150 miles away. The "brook of the Arabah" (6:14, RSV) was a wadi (gully) associated with the Dead Sea.

So ends the main collection of utterances by Amos which constitute the first six chapters of the book. A different type of presentation characterizes the remainder of Amos' work. The prophet has unfolded the plan of God for Israel, reminding the nation of her sin, pleading with unrepentant leaders, and preparing the nation for the inevitable end. He has dealt with errors within society and within the religious system of the day. He has refused to spare the feelings of those most guilty in riding roughshod over the less fortunate. With increasing clarity and intensity, he has reached the sad and somber conclusion that only destruction and captivity lie ahead.

The experience of Israel should speak to our generation concerning the truth of the axiom, "Pride goeth before destruction, and an haughty spirit before a fall" (Prov. 16:18). Even a cursory glance at our national temper shows the increasing pride in our accomplishments. The achievements in space exploration, atomic research, and other areas of science have produced a glorification of man and his abilities. Such scientific achievements have added to the image of boastfulness with which America is characterized by other nations.

Man's pride cannot remain unrelated to God, since pride is man's assertion of his self-sufficiency. Once the sense of dependence is lost, pride toward God is the ultimate outcome. The wise man is the one who recognizes his own ignorance and relies upon the wisdom of God. Such a person walks humbly before God and refuses to demonstrate a haughty spirit toward others.

Coupled with this amplification of man's pride is the sharp decline of moral conscience, even as the two were complementary in ancient Israel. Since World War II there has been a disastrous degree of moral deterioration. Ameri-

ca's conscience, once quickened by the Christian ethic, has
steadily become swallowed up in humanistic pride. Only
by the breaking of pride's stranglehold and the substitution
of insight concerning God's righteousness can there be long-
term hope for our land.

FOR CLASS PREPARATION

1. Placing yourself in the position of Samaria's leaders, consider
   the natural reactions to Amos' message and examine the process
   of rationalizing which accompanies such a defensive position.
2. List factors at work in our society which cause indifference to
   the needs of others. Seek to determine whether these factors
   have lulled your church into a state of "at ease in Zion."
3. Analyze critically the increasing pride in man's achievements
   and consider seriously God's reaction to pride (cf. Amos 6:8;
   Prov. 11:2; 16:5; 21:4; 26:12; Isa. 2:11; Luke 14:7–11;
   18:9–14; 1 Cor. 4:6–7; James 4:6; 1 Peter 5:5–6).

FOR ADVANCED STUDY

1. For further information on the city of Samaria:
   G. E. Wright, *Biblical Archaeology* (Rev. Ed., 1962), pp. 152–155.
   G. W. VanBeek, "Samaria," *The Interpreter's Dictionary of the
   Bible,* R–Z, 182–188.
2. For information on the musical instruments referred to by Amos:
   S. R. Driver, *Joel and Amos* (Cambridge Bible), pp. 234–236.
3. For a description of ancient siege operations:
   G. E. Wright, *Biblical Archaeology,* (Rev. Ed., 1962) pp. 167–171.
   J. W. Wevers, "War, Methods of," *The Interpreter's Dictionary of
   the Bible,* R–Z, 801–805.
4. For a discussion of problems in interpreting 6:9–10:
   E. A. Edghill, *The Book of Amos* (Westminster Commentaries),
   pp. 65–66.
   G. A. Smith, *The Book of the Twelve Prophets,* pp. 184–187.
5. For an analysis of the geographical limits of the projected oppression
   in 6:14:
   R. S. Cripps, *The Book of Amos,* pp. 304–306.

---

[1] John Bright, *The Kingdom of God* (New York: Abingdon Press,
1953), p. 69.

CHAPTER 8

TEACHING BY SYMBOLS—AMOS 7-8

I. THE VISION OF LOCUST PLAGUE (7:1-3)
1. The Invasion of the Locusts (7:1-2a)
2. The Plea by Amos (7:2b)
3. The Response of God (7:3)

II. THE VISION OF FIRE (7:4-6)
1. The Devouring Fire (7:4)
2. The Plea by Amos (7:5)
3. The Response of God (7:6)

III. THE VISION OF THE PLUMB LINE (7:7-9)
1. The Dramatic Scene (7:7-8a)
2. The Meaning of the Event (7:8b-9)

IV. REACTION AT BETHEL (7:10-17)
1. The Charge Against Amos (7:10-11)
2. The Command of Amaziah (7:12-13)
3. The Answer by Amos (7:14-17)

V. THE VISION OF THE BASKET OF SUMMER FRUIT (8:1-3)
1. An Ordinary Basket of Fruit (8:1-2a)
2. An Extraordinary Interpretation (8:2b-3)

VI. THE RENDEZVOUS WITH DOOM (8:4-14)
1. The Basic Causes (8:4-6)
2. The Bitter Day (8:7-14)

8

Teaching by Symbols

AMOS 7–8

IS IT TRUE that a picture is worth a thousand words? Is it possible to condense a message into a terse word picture and still relate the depth of the experience? Nothing is more difficult in the art of communication than presenting a deep psychic experience in language that can be understood by all men. Long before the time of Amos, actual pictures were used as a primitive means of communication. Slowly this pictographic form gave way to the alphabet method. Even then the original pictures were preserved in the letters of the alphabet. Furthermore, this linkage with simple pictures gave a sense of concreteness to the language which Amos inherited. While abstractions were possible, they were rare. Even proper names bore readily recognized meanings.

By means of terse word pictures, Amos was able to translate for his hearers and readers some of his deepest experiences with God. His mode of presentation, the vision, was more than just another literary device. This form of expressing truth was similar in many ways to the recounting of a dream. However, the powers of intuition and imagination were heightened beyond the normal scope of a dream. Images and ideas, both old and new, were combined in unique ways to present vivid pictures. Almost without exception the imagery was drawn from the surroundings with which the prophet was most familiar. S. R. Driver has summarized these factors, saying:

> In other words, the vision may be described as a combination into new forms, under the influence of a determining impulse, of the images and impressions with which the mind,

through its waking experience, is stored. In a prophetic vision, the determining impulse will have been due to the operation of the revealing Spirit; . . . The Vision is thus the forcible symbolic presentation of a prophetic truth.[1]

I. THE VISION OF LOCUST PLAGUE (7:1–3)

This is the first of three visions which formed a unit and were probably presented in the order found here. Two further visions, recorded after the historical interlude concerning Bethel's response to Amos' preaching, stood in a line of progression with the first unit. It may well be that they were added one at the time on separate occasions after Amos was driven out of Bethel. The progression of thought is obvious since the fourth vision rests upon the foundation of the first three, and the fifth on the first four.

John Watts has suggested: "There is a finality about this fourth vision which rings true only when the intercession and struggle of the others is presupposed." [2] Much the same may be said about the fifth vision. In all five visions, there is an introduction, a description of what is seen or heard, and a concluding statement concerning God's attitude and the role of the prophet Amos.

1. The Invasion of the Locusts (7:1–2a)

Amos first saw the beginning of a dread event for the whole community of Israel: the forming by God of a host of locusts. The wording used showed the locusts in the larval stage; then suddenly they had grown to maturity and finished eating all the foliage. The whole process from larva to devastation was described in a few phrases. The catastrophic nature of the event was clearly shown by reference to the "latter growth after the king's mowings" (7:1). This was a critical time in that the spring rains were past and the crops available for the people were destroyed. While the tribute to the king had been paid, there was no hope for the private Israelite since the intense summer heat was just beginning.

2. The Plea by Amos (7:2b)

This intercession on behalf of Israel demonstrated the love and compassion of the rugged prophet from Tekoa. Beneath the stern exterior was a deep concern for God's people. Speaking for the nation, he cried out for God's forgiveness with obvious hope that the reality of the vision could be averted. Amos saw that the nation, though proud and arrogant, could never arise again. In the light of such potential calamity, she was only a small and helpless people.

3. The Response of God (7:3)

In answer to prophetic intercession, God promised that this calamity (vv. 1–2) would not occur. Such a change of intent presented no difficulty to the ancient Hebrew nor did the use of the verb translated "repent" in relation to God's activity. However, in the light of Christian teachings, the very idea of God repenting appears to be out of keeping with his revealed character. The word here used does not carry the idea of moral turning but the concept of sorrow or regret in relation to an event or a series of events. There is clearly in this context a change of mind and a redirection of purpose. Israel does not escape except as regards this particular punishment. There is here the belief that God does respond to the pleas of his people. E. A. Edghill points out this aspect of God's response to men, as he says:

> This anthropomorphic expression, which appears so frequently in the sacred writers, bears witness to their belief in a God who cares, a God who answers prayer, and can control all things for His purposes of righteousness and love: He can be moved by man's appeal, because His will for man's good is unchangable.[3]

II. THE VISION OF FIRE (7:4-6)

A second visionary experience presented another dire calamity as evident punishment upon Israel. Again the vision was introduced by the statement, "Thus the Lord God showed me" (7:4, RSV; cf. 7:1, 7; 8:1). Amos never missed an opportunity to present God as a revealing God, one who reveals his secret counsel to his servants the prophets "He revealeth his secret unto his servants the prophets" (3:7).

1. *The Devouring Fire* (7:4)

In this vision, God summoned fire as the instrument of his judgment. The idea of "contending by fire" probably included the imagery of a controversy ending in an all-inclusive destructive conflagration. While the verse may refer symbolically to an invasion by the Assyrians, the more reasonable explanation would lie in an actual fire. It seems that Amos saw a fire appearing in field and forest and sweeping across the land, completely out of control. The drying up of the subterranean waters described both the intensity and the utter destructive power of the fire. The natural result would be a drought like man had never known, a judgment even more severe than that of the locusts.

2. *The Plea by Amos* (7:5)

Again Amos sought mercy from God, acting in behalf of his people about to be punished. His plea was identical to his previously successful intercession, except for the change of one word. Instead of requesting God to "forgive," he asked him to "cease" his destructive work. The scene must have been so vividly awful as to prompt an outcry of horror without relation to Israel's moral condition. The plea was kin to a spontaneous command, "stop!"

3. *The Response of God* (7:6)

While some writers would charge Amos with presumption or familiarity, God was pictured as graciously accepting his plea. Once again the prophet's intercession accomplished the withdrawal of this catastrophe as an instrument of judgment. God had changed his intention, as far as Israel was concerned, in response to the heartfelt prayer of his servant.

III. The Vision of the Plumb Line (7:7–9)

One of the basic implements for the construction of buildings has always been the plumb line. This is simply a weight tied to the end of a string which will indicate a true perpendicular relationship to the earth. By such a device a wall can be tested, both during construction and at a later date, against an invariable standard. If the wall leans to an appreciable extent, it must be declared unsafe and thus must either be straightened or torn down.

1. The Dramatic Scene (7:7–8a)

Amos used the imagery of the plumb line procedure to present another scene of judgment. Here the prophet did not see the disaster itself but the reason for the coming punishment. It was no ordinary carpenter whom he saw in his vision; rather it was God himself who stood with plumb line in hand. As the master builder he was checking a wall originally built to the proper standard. Amos responded to the simple question "What do you see?" with a similar type of answer as he said, "A plumb line." Neither the question nor the answer appeared to be profound. However, the very simplicity of the whole sequence implied that a profound assertion would follow, preparing a dramatic setting for the message.

2. The Meaning of the Event (7:8b–9)

This ordinary construction procedure, made special by the presence of God, pointed toward an infinitely more important measurement by God. He stood as the builder of Israel, ready to test the character of the nation. The plumb line represented his own revealed righteousness as the standard by which his people must be judged. His procedure of testing was in no way arbitrary but was based upon his own absolute standard of righteousness. He could not be accused of sighting by eye or making an educated guess. Rather, he stood with line in hand, ready to demonstrate to all the world how "out of plumb" was the nation Israel.

Amos had no opportunity to plead for his people as he had done when confronted by the previous visions. Before he could voice a plea, God pronounced with authority and certainty that he would not "again pass by them any more" (7:8). They had failed the crucial moral test in that they did not conform to the standard of his will. Forgiveness of the nation was thus beyond the immediate hope for prophet and people. Since the only alternative was judgment, three symbols of Israel's moral degradation were pointed out as objects of destruction.

(1) *The high places.*—These were not singled out because they stood in competition to the Temple at Jerusalem. For centuries, the Israelites had gathered at these religious sites, usually situated on natural or artificial hills near the major towns and cities. In all probability, the Canaanites had previously worshiped at some of these same "holy sites." Amos did not condemn the place of worship, nor did he claim they were worshiping the wrong god. His concern throughout the book was related to the improper concept of God's character and what God desired from his people. As far as Israel could understand, God only required a set number of sacrifices, feasts, and pilgrimages—nothing more!

(2) *The sanctuaries.*—In parallel poetic construction, the local sanctuaries, such as the one at Bethel, were also labeled for destruction. While the high places were primarily open-air shrines with an altar, pillars, and sacred stones, the sanctuaries were probably distinguished by buildings in the form of a special house of worship. For Amos, these were further symbols of the amoral, and at times immoral, character of the worship by Israel.

(3) *The house of Jeroboam.*—Along with the religious structures, the royal administration was designated as an object of destruction. While Amos never condemned the private or religious life of the king, he did view his dynasty as coming to an end. This may have been viewed as attendant upon the end of the nation, or it may have been more specific. Very possibly Amos realized the potential internal strife which would characterize the final days of Israel.

Actually, the dynasty of Jeroboam ended shortly after the public ministry of Amos. At that time Jeroboam's son Zechariah was assassinated after only six months in office as king.

These three visions of Amos can still speak their word to the present age. The first two, dealing with locust and fire, appear to be out of the scope of life today. While locusts attack certain areas occasionally and forest fires ravage many acres of timberland each year, the application of these events as judgment is not always clear. However, the manner in which Amos interceded for his people points to an indispensable prerequisite for the modern prophet. Anyone who would bring God's message, whether of judgment or salvation, must enter upon the task with genuine sympathy and compassion, having first interceded in agonizing prayer.

The third vision, concerning the plumb line, has more obvious application to modern society. Men and nations are still measured by the standard of God's righteousness. While salvation comes through the gift of God's grace, the demands of righteousness are infinitely heightened by the revelation of God in Christ. The use of the plumb line is still justified imagery for God's insistence upon righteous living on the part of his children. Judgment awaits the nation or individual who ignores this relationship to the righteous Judge.

IV. REACTION AT BETHEL (7:10-17)

The clear statement of the prophet brought response from the priest at the sanctuary, since he had probably longed for something concrete with which to charge Amos. Having no spiritual resources with which to defeat Amos, Amaziah was quick to grasp the opportunity to use the prophet's words concerning the king. The whole passage, although possibly only a fragment of a longer history of Amos' ministry, was introduced at the most suitable point in the book. The closing words of Amos were picked up by

Amaziah, conveying the spirit of the clash between prophet and priest.

1. *The Charge Against Amos* (7:10–11)

By careful exaggeration and subtle innuendo, Amaziah was able to charge Amos with conspiracy against the throne and the nation. Actually Amos had not acted or spoken in a treasonable way toward anyone in governmental authority. He had neither made an attempt on the king's life nor sought to lead others to do so. However, it must be fairly stated that Amaziah had some cause for his concern in that previous prophets had been associated with revolutionary activity. Ahijah had been involved in the rebellion of Jeroboam I (1 Kings 11:29–40), while Elisha had played a leading role in the affairs which brought Jehu to the throne (2 Kings 9:1–3).

The report by Amaziah included several interesting things about the effect of Amos' ministry. Certainly the prophet could never complain that his voice was not being heard since Amaziah could report that "the land is not able to bear all his words" (7:10). Such was the report from his own generation, not a later estimate of his impact. The fact that Amos is mentioned by name without qualifying description must indicate that he was well known even to the king. The fact that Amaziah could quote (or almost quote) the words of Amos indicates that his words were reaching the leaders who most needed to hear the message.

2. *The Command of Amaziah* (7:12–13)

After filing his report with the king, Amaziah took matters into his own hands. Whether he had received support or directions from the king was not mentioned. The basis of his authority resided in the fact that he was the priest of "the king's sanctuary" (RSV). This sense of royal patronage to the sacred precincts at Bethel is significant. Rather than being the house of God, the sanctuary belonged to the king.

Amaziah's command was simply for Amos to get out of the

country and take his prophesying with him. The reference
to Amos as a seer rather than a prophet may relate to the
preceding visions or may have been a touch of irony. Certainly there is irony in the suggestion that Amos seek his
bread (his pay) in Judah where the people would enjoy
hearing his condemnation of the Northern Kingdom.

3. The Answer by Amos (7:14–17)

Remarkably concise was the defense by the prophet in
his own behalf. He first denied that he was a part of the
prophetic guilds of his day. Next, he clearly stated his occupation as a herdsman and a cultivator of sycamore trees.
Finally, he asserted that his authority was in the distinct call
he had received of God to be his prophet to Israel. The
double use of "the Lord" in verse 15 emphasizes that no
one else had made him a prophet—neither king nor his own
desire. While he admitted his function as a prophet, Amos
denied being the type of prophet which Amaziah had in
mind. The real point of his defense was the source of his
authority rather than his occupation.

Without hesitation, Amos reiterated and amplified the
doom which God had promised for Israel. In no way did he
modify or withdraw his previous assertions but rather
planted his feet firmly and reaffirmed, "Thus saith the Lord."
The imagery behind verse 17 suggests a vision of a captured
city in which the conquerors defile Amaziah's wife, kill his
children, and divide up his property. Amos pictured
Amaziah finally dying in a foreign land along with the exiled
nation. By these harsh and realistic words, Amos both reaffirmed his previous messages and assured Amaziah that
he would not escape, even with royal patronage and priestly
status.

The clash between Amos and Amaziah was just one skir-
mish in a long battle between institutional religion and the
voice of dissent. How often the prophetic voices of constructive criticism have been silenced in the name of a man,
a king, or a denomination! Institutional religion is always
quick to brand as heresy any corrective criticism and slow to

examine itself through self-criticism. While the state-church image immediately comes to mind, the ills represented by Amaziah are not limited to an established or dominant church. Wherever the prophetic is swallowed up by the official or experiential religion is squelched by tradition, it becomes difficult for God's Spirit to work through his children.

While the voice of dissent is too often classed as heresy or irresponsibility, it is also too frequently viewed as irrelevant. This appears to be the easiest way to write off that which does not agree with the prejudices of an established group. R. L. Honeycutt states well the evasive tactics so frequently used against prophetic preaching:

> This attitude is confronted on a contemporary basis when one hears such statements as: "preachers ought to preach the gospel and leave other issues alone," or "the church doesn't have any business in politics" (or racial tensions, or anything else except the maintenance of the status quo). Inevitably, there is always the Amaziah who, while he may not deny the right to prophesy, indicates that it should be done in other locales, in other social situations, or in other religious structures. The more rigid the institutionalism, the greater the insistence that prophetic religion is irrelevant both to geographical locale and to the situation at hand.[4]

A careful study of the ministry of Amos and the other prophets should cause us to hesitate in reasoned and prayerful reflection before evaluating the voice of prophetic preaching in our midst. While there is unmistakable finality in the mission of Christ, who among us can claim finality in either the full understanding of the gospel or the ramifications of the gospel message for our day?

V. The Vision of the Basket of Summer Fruit (8:1–3)

Yet another vision was added to the accumulative effect of the three visions interrupted by the clash with Amaziah. One cannot be certain whether this vision was spoken by Amos after the order to leave Bethel was given. It may have been presented at a later time or added by Amos to the written form of his messages. While the third vision promised that the doom was certain, this vision declared it to be final.

1. An Ordinary Basket of Fruit (8:1–2a)

Nothing could be more ordinary than a basket of fruit resting on the ground of the marketplace. Other men had looked upon a similar sight with no more question than "How much?" Somehow Amos was looking at the same type of object with a definite feeling of seeing something more. The difference lay in the spiritual perception of the prophet from Tekoa and in the fact that God was causing him to see the deeper meaning below the level of normal conscious attention.

2. An Extraordinary Interpretation (8:2b–3)

The meaning of the vision was implied in the description of the basket as containing summer fruit. This was the fruit which ripened toward the end of the summer and was gathered in early autumn. It may well be that Amos could see this fruit as the last of the crop, the end of the agricultural year. In the reply by God to the answer of Amos, the linkage was made in sound as well as sight, the two key words being "summer fruit" (*qayits*) and "end" (*qets*). By this dual association, the end was pronounced for Israel in dread finality. Even as God had yielded twice to the intercessions of Amos, he had twice repeated the irrevocable nature of judgment. By means of three lamentations (verse 3), Amos drove home the shocking effect of the final collapse of the nation. There would be wailing, mounds of corpses, and eventually a ghastly silence hovering over the land.

VI. The Rendezvous with Doom (8:4–14)

Few, if any, who heard Amos preach could doubt that he believed with all his being that doom was coming for the nation Israel. Why then did he find it necessary to repeat over and over again the pessimistic warnings of judgment to come? In the first place, many of his messages are in fragmentary form and may have been delivered on separate occasions. In fact, the passage at hand may have been delivered prior to his expulsion from Bethel since it echoes much that is found in chapters 1-6. Some of the material may have been spoken in Judah and included in the written form of his labors. It is probable that he emphasized his themes of judgment and social justice to several groups on separate occasions and at different locations. Each time he would be sure to point out these emphases which were the hallmark of his divine call.

1. The Basic Causes (8:4-6)

The proposed end for the proud kingdom was not without cause. In the light of the list of flagrant sins which were included throughout the book, Amos did not have to look very hard for justification concerning his position. Rather, the fruits of unrighteousness were everywhere evident for one who was in touch with the righteous God. In this passage Amos concentrated upon the sins of the trading community, those merchants who came into most frequent contact with the poor and the outcast.

(1) *Oppression of the poor and needy* (8:4).—In parallel construction, treatment of the less fortunates was generalized. The act of swallowing up (trampling, RSV) the needy could have taken many forms, some of which were specified in the verses which follow. A similar charge was made by the prophet in 2:7 where the King James Version used the idea of "panting after." The imagery may be that of a wild animal panting after its prey. The second general charge concerned the manner in which the merchants would force the poor to a premature end by their unscrupulous practices.

(2) *Impatience over the festivals* (8:5a).—Amos pointed out the worldliness of the merchants who chafed at the interruption which holy days brought to their profits. They longed for the sabbath and New Moon Festival to end so they could be back about "business as usual." Here Amos

was emphasizing the superficiality of these men who threatened the spirit of the sabbath as well as the well-being of the helpless.

(3) *Dishonesty in weights and measures* (8:5b).—Three methods of cheating the public were mentioned, two of which are easily explained. The first concerned the ephah, a measure for grain equaling about eight gallons. By the use of a false bottom or by reducing the size of the vessel, the merchant could increase his profit. The second method involved the shekel, a unit of weight, which could be made heavier in order to require the buyer to place more silver on the balances. The third method may relate to the rigging of the balances so as to falsify the amount placed on the scales, or it may refer to the general practice of deceit. At the end of verse 6, Amos mentioned another evidence of dishonesty not connected with weights or measures. The selling of the "refuse of the wheat" designated the inferior grain mixed with the chaff which was sold to the poor.

(4) *Buying of debtors* (8:6).—Not only did the merchants take advantage of the poor and needy but they took into servitude a man, his children, or his entire family as discharge of a debt. In describing how little regarded were human values, Amos referred to the trade of silver for human life, an act sometimes involving no more than the price of a pair of sandals. This same idea was expressed in 2:6 where the context could refer to the bribery of corrupt judges or the selling of debtors into slavery by greedy creditors. Here the context seems to demand application to the merchants as creditors.

What a field day Amos would have in regard to similar ills of our society. Not only are the poor always with us, they are exploited in much the same way. A man may find himself "swallowed up" by creditors who present Utopian opportunities to buy more than he can afford or to consolidate all his debts into one larger debt. Balloon payments, commissions, fees, interest, insurance, and fine print may result in the loss of possessions long paid for. The selling of inferior merchandise or practice of dishonesty in weights and packaging would still shock Amos. The complaining about sabbath observance, or the ignoring of it, might send Amos back to the peace and solitude of ancient Israel.

2. The Bitter Day (8:7-14)

Although Amos often emphasized the horrors of siege and conquest, he was by no means limited to the imagery drawn from such events. Israel was about to meet her downfall on the field of battle, but her rendezvous with doom would involve far more than military defeat. Another oath by God, based upon the pride of Jacob, acted as a seal concerning the validity of Amos' words.

(1) *A time of natural calamity* (8:7-9).—The terrible judgment to come was described in terms of vivid hyperboles related to two events in nature which always caused extreme dread among the ancients. The trembling of the earth, like the rise and fall of the floods along the Nile River in Egypt, probably described the convulsions of an earthquake. The darkening of the sun at noon, with attendant darkness even on a clear day, probably related to an eclipse of the sun similar to that seen in Palestine in 763 B.C. Amos' statement concerning the Day of the Lord being darkness rather than light (5:18,20) takes on even more meaning here.

(2) *A time of mourning* (8:10).—Such alarming spectacles would rule out any thought of joy and pleasure. Festival pilgrimages would be turned into parades of mourning while songs of praise would be transformed into sorrowful lamentations. The use of sackcloth and the shaving of one's head were signs of great grief in ancient cultures. The end result would be sounds of intense mourning like that shown in the most bitter lamentations when an only son was taken by death.

(3) *A time of spiritual hunger* (8:11-14).—The people of Israel knew well the fear associated with times of famine and drought, as well as the ravages of these disasters. The

prophet, however, turned their attention to another type of hunger—the desire for spiritual bread and water. While the people were indifferent to God's word in their midst in the present situation of prosperity and peace, there would come the day when they would be eager to hear that word of God. Yet, they would wander aimlessly without finding a prophet who could share the counsel of God with them. In such a time, even the young people who were best equipped to survive would fail for lack of sustenance. The false worship at Bethel, Dan, and Beersheba would prove of no help. Swearing by such superficial substitutes for true worship could not avert the sad judgment that "they shall fall, and never rise up again" (8:14).

How applicable these words are for Americans who spend so much time seeking substitutes for God. They never find satisfaction. Almost invariably, there comes a time in the life of every individual when a word from God would be welcome. Yet, in all too many cases, the famine has taken its toll. The person has spurned too long the things of God and knows neither how to seek God nor where his word for our day may be found. One cannot miss the relevance of Isaiah's words: "Seek ye the Lord while he may be found, call ye upon him while he is near" (Isa. 55:6). While the privilege of knowing God may long be available to modern man, there is always the possibility that it may not be so.

FOR CLASS PREPARATION

1. Use a Bible dictionary to gain more information on the locust invasions of ancient times in order to make more realistic the pattern of Amos' visions.
2. Employing the imagery of Amos' vision of the plumb line, compare your own life against the standard of God's righteousness as seen in the Scriptures, especially in the life and ministry of Christ.
3. Analyze the oft-repeated saying, "Preachers ought to preach the gospel and leave other issues alone." Consider seriously the extent of application which the gospel has for our day.

For Advanced Study

1. For a discussion of prophetic visions:
   R. S. Cripps, *The Book of Amos*, pp. 87–101.
   S. R. Driver, *Joel and Amos* (Cambridge Bible), pp. 200–201.
   J. D. W. Watts, *Vision and Prophecy in Amos*, pp. 27–50.
2. For an understanding of the relation between prophets and priests:
   H. W. Robinson, *Inspiration and Revelation in the Old Testament*, pp. 222–230.
3. For a comparison of institutional and experiential religion:
   R. L. Honeycutt, *Amos and His Message*, pp. 132–144.

---

[1] S. R. Driver (ed.), *The Cambridge Bible for Schools and Colleges: The Books of Joel and Amos* (Cambridge: University Press, 1901), XXV, 201.

[2] John D. Watts, *Vision and Prophecy in Amos* (Grand Rapids, Michigan: Wm. B. Eerdmans, 1958), p. 31.

[3] Edghill, *The Book of Amos* (2nd ed.; London: Methuen and Co., rev. ed., 1926), p. 72.

[4] R. L. Honeycutt, *Amos and His Message* (Nashville: Broadman Press, 1963), p. 136.

CHAPTER 9

HOPE FOR THE FUTURE—AMOS 9

9

Hope for the Future

How TRAGIC would have been the story of God's dealing with Israel if the message ended with the words: "They shall fall, and never rise again" (8:14, RSV). All that remained would have been the historian's account of the invading armies of the Assyrians conquering, destroying, pillaging, and carrying captive the inhabitants. Less than forty years later he could have recorded for posterity the siege of Samaria and its fall. He could have pronounced the verdict, Finished. However, the story of God's concern for Israel involved hope as well as doom. This chapter completes the picture by combining both of these elements to demonstrate God's love even within the framework of his judgment.

I. THE VISION OF THE SMITTEN SANCTUARY (9:1-4)

The fifth vision seen by Amos added to the other four and was built upon them. It served to make final many of the pronouncements concerning Israel's superficial worship patterns which were a large part of Amos' burden. Seemingly, Amos was a part of the worshiping throng at the Bethel sanctuary, or else previous experiences there served as a background. Notice that the prophet was not caused to see an object which demanded interpretation; rather, the scene was all set and required only his attention.

1. The Destruction of the Sanctuary (9:1a)

Looking about him, Amos saw the people gathered for a high hour of worship. Like the other worshipers, he could see the altar as the focus point of attention. Yet, once again

117

he could see more in the ordinary course of events—God himself seemed to be standing beside (or upon) the altar. Then the command to destroy the building was given by God: "Smite the capitals until the thresholds shake, and shatter them on the heads of all the people" (9:1a, RSV). The agent of God's judgment was not specified nor was the actual destruction described. While Amos left unfulfilled but certain the completion of the act, the method was quite specific, since the smiting of the capitals (the ornamental part of the pillars which supported the roof) would cause the roof to tumble in upon the crowd.

This vision paralleled in essence the destruction of the Temple of Dagon, when Samson brought the building down upon the Philistines (Judg. 16:23-30). It was said of Samson that he "grasped the two middle pillars upon which the house rested, and he leaned his weight upon them, his right hand on the one and his left hand on the other. . . . Then he bowed with all his might; and the house fell upon the lords and upon all the people that were in it" (Judg. 16:29-30, RSV).

2. *The Impossibility of Escape* (9:1b-4)

The completeness of the destruction was indelibly impressed upon Amos by repeated warnings that no one would escape. Lest any one should miss the threefold pronouncement of doom to all involved in the sanctuary worship, Amos recalled ways in which men might expect to escape. Even digging down into Sheol, the abode of the dead, or climbing up to the heights of the heaven would be useless. Mount Carmel was singled out as a seemingly good (but useless) place for hiding from the wrath of God. In biblical times, the top of Carmel was thickly wooded, and the slopes were pitted by hundreds of caves.

Another extreme example, the bottom of the sea, would prove to be equally futile as a hiding place. The reference to the serpent was drawn from the generally held view in ancient thought that a great monster had his home at the bottom of the sea. Amos used the imagery to emphasize that no place on earth was beyond the control and concern of God. Even being carried captive into a foreign land would not protect those designated for destruction. How strongly Amos felt the omnipresence of God! Nothing on earth, within the recesses of the earth, in the depths of the sea, or in heaven itself could escape the judgment decreed.

A Christian cannot read these words of Amos without recalling parallel figures of speech used by Paul. "Who shall separate us from the love of Christ? shall tribulation, or distress, or persecution, or famine, or nakedness, or peril, or sword? . . . For I am persuaded, that neither death, nor life, nor angels, nor principalities, nor powers, nor things present, nor things to come, nor height, nor depth, nor any other creature, shall be able to separate us from the love of God, which is in Christ Jesus our Lord" (Rom. 8:35, 38–39). How striking are the similarities, but how different are the expressions of God's concern. For Amos, God expressed his concern through judgment. Paul saw in Christ the same omnipresence of God's love. Do the words of Paul negate the insights of Amos, or are both two aspects of God's concern for man? For those within the will of God, who have found their place in the new covenant, there is no escape from God's love. However, for those outside the will of God, like favored Israel of old, there is no hiding place from his judgment. The nation or the individual which refuses to measure life by God's standard of righteousness will find judgment inescapable.

II. The Sequel to the Vision (9:5–7)

Although the vision proper appears to end with verse 4, the following verses stand in close agreement with the vision. There is first a third doxology (9:5–6) which parallels in form those found in 4:13 and 5:8–9, employing the same striking hymnodic style. The idea, previously expressed, that these doxologies may be fragments of an old hymn seems reasonable in this context as well. There follows an impressive statement of God's providential relations with other nations which goes far beyond the usual bounds of Israelite nationalism (9:7).

1. The Majesty of God (9:5–6)

The idea of God's judgment as inescapable seemed to demand some confirmation for the average Israelite. No greater appeal could be found than the majesty of God as creator and ruler of all nature, the one controlling earth, the heavens, and the rain. The idea of his melting the earth by his touch may refer either to the bringing of drought or to volcanic activity. The action was viewed as catastrophic to the extent that all should mourn. The rising and falling of the earth may well relate to the power of an earthquake (see 8:8). God's creation and control reached to the very limits of the heavens, even to the great vault of the sky. From the heavens he controlled the life-giving rains which he poured out upon the earth.

Such a view of God's control of the universe certainly underscores his ability to seek out those who might try to escape his judgment. Scientific explanations of the phenomena appealed to in such passages as this do not rule out the concept that God controls that which he has created. Rather, the greater depth of understanding should increase the awareness that "the heavens declare the glory of God; and the firmament sheweth his handywork" (Psalm 19:1).

2. The Providence of God (9:7)

The proud nation of Israel had long appealed for preferential treatment on the basis of being chosen people of God. Many Israelites must have rejected Amos' words of doom on this basis. Amos met such an objection by describing it as another form of escapism. In the light of Israel's moral failure, she had forfeited her place in the divine economy of God. She stood in the same relation to God as did the distant Ethiopians who lived in the remote region of the upper Nile Valley.

Not only were the faraway Ethiopians on equal status

with Israel, the traditional enemies of Israel were objects of God's favor. An important point of pride for the Israelites was God's special act in bringing their forefathers out of Egypt. Yet, even this claim of uniqueness was destroyed by the assertion that God had a hand in bringing the Philistines from their homeland (Crete or possibly Asia Minor) and the Syrians from their original home in the distant northeast.

This important verse goes far beyond a negative statement of rejection for Israel. There is here a view of God's relation to all men which paved the way for further prophetic insight. Amos is asserting here that God is Lord over all human history and that all men are equal in his sight. By this, he implies that any other nation could stand in the same place of privilege which Israel had known. Both God's concern in love and his concern in judgment are without discrimination. Neither geographical limitations nor race matter in the least when God seeks to accomplish his purpose.

III. THE PRESERVATION OF A REMNANT (9:8-10)

The darkness of the storm clouds in the earlier chapters of Amos become increasingly evident as the light begins to break through. It is always difficult to understand the bleakness of a message of doom without the contrast which is presented by a dream of hope. The whole tenor of the book changes at this point in just such a dramatic way.

1. A Glimmer of Hope (9:8)

The extreme contrast between darkness and light was sharply and suddenly drawn within one verse. The former pronouncements were summed up in the words, "Behold, the eyes of the Lord God are upon the sinful kingdom, and I will destroy it from the surface of the ground" (9:8a, RSV). Nothing could sound more irrevocable! And yet the bright side appeared with the words, "Except that I will not utterly destroy the house of Jacob, says the Lord" (9:8b, RSV). Although the judgment had not been averted and the sentence had not been withdrawn, there was hope in the fact that Israel's ruin was not irreparable.

A careful examination of the verses which follow will raise serious questions as to the author of the remainder of the chapter. It must be admitted that the words seem to come through the personality of someone other than the stern, unwavering prophet from Tekoa. The sudden change from doom to hope without stated reasons appears quite different from the previous pattern of Amos. The fact that the dream of a future prosperity (9:11-15) is devoid of moral considerations does not sound natural to a prophet with the moral conscience of Amos. On the other hand, it must also be stated that God's Spirit could have moved Amos to see such hope after his public appearances in Israel. His vision of the future would then be a projection of an ideal Israel, purified by the destruction of the kingdom and the exile. This would certainly be in keeping with the combined message of judgment and hope seen in the writing of the other great prophets of Israel.

The question raised is not one of authenticity but authorship. If God led a later writer to complete the message begun by Amos, there is no real question of inspiration. To claim that God could not speak through later generations would be to limit by human reason the infinite freedom of God to accomplish his purposes.

While it is impossible to decide this issue for all time, in these words God is still speaking—either through Amos or another prophet.

2. A Sifting of Israel (9:9-10)

In these verses, the meaning of the exile changed from doom to discipline. Instead of being swallowed up by the nations, Israel would be sifted by the familiar to and fro motion of one shaking a sieve. The result would be a purging type of judgment by means of which a purified remnant would be preserved. While the meaning of the sifting seems clear, the type of sieve used in the analogy remains obscure.

At least two types were used for sifting grain in ancient times. One type allowed the chaff to pass through, retaining the grain while another permitted the grain to fall, keeping pebbles in the sieve. The two operations are pictured by the King James Version and Revised Standard Version, respectively. Retained is the grain in the former and the pebbles in the latter. Regardless of the method, the result is the same: A remnant, composed of the faithful servants of God, is separated and spared from destruction.

The sinners, pictured as destined for certain destruction, were characterized as misguided optimists who denied that evil would ever come to them. Relying upon privileged status, they were all too certain that everything would work out their way. Violent death was to be the reward of their self-sufficient pride.

IV. THE PROMISE OF A NEW DAY (9:11-15)

The fortunes of Israel had reached such a low ebb in the prophecies of destruction and exile that the only outlook had to be upward. The one thing which could affect the humiliation of defeat and enslavement would be the dream of a new day brighter than anything ever realized previously by God's people. It must be understood that the dream of restoration presupposed the disciplinary sifting of Israel during the exile, by means of which a purified people would share the brighter future.

1. *Restoration of the Kingdom of David* (9:11-12)

Hope for the future took the familiar form of memory concerning better days in the past. Since no ruler, past or present, rivaled David in the popular mind, the golden age of David often became the symbol of greater things yet to be. Although such memories lingered deep in the heart of the Israelites, there was nothing left but a humble structure called a booth (RSV) or tabernacle (KJV). The word, describing a hut of branches, was also used of temporary shelters for soldiers and workmen as well as sheds for cattle.

Even this was fallen! The repairing and rebuilding of
David's house symbolized the process of restoration by
which Israel would live again.

Since the greatness of David's reign lay also in the extent
of his kingdom, renewal must also include the repossession
of territory once ruled by him. Not only Edom, an especially
persistent foe of Israel, but all the nations belonging to the
old kingdom were included. The idea of nations being called
by the name of the Lord implied ownership or conquest
in his name. The people of such nations were considered
to be the possessions of the Lord in a special way.

2. Renewal of the Land and People (9:13–15)

Life in the future is further idealized by a series of hyperboles picturing ultimate fertility, prosperity, and happiness.
The first picture describes graphically an agricultural cycle
in which the normally separate tasks would overlap. Because
of the abundance of the crops, the workers would overtake
one another: The one harvesting would still be gathering
when the one plowing for the next season came along; the
task of pressing the grapes would not be completed when
sowing began for the next year. It is possible that this may
refer to the speeding up of the ripening process rather than
the abundance of the crops. Such expectations for better
times stand in sharp contrast to Amos' words concerning
drought, blight, famine, and earthquakes as agents of God's
judgment (4:6–11). Here it is God who blesses with the
same intensity with which he judged his people. The unlimited potentials of God's power are dramatically presented by means of the very opposite of his warnings and
judgments. Instead of the hills melting because of God's
anger, they would flow with the produce of the vineyards
upon their slopes and melt (literally, dissolve themselves)
by the abundance of the harvest.

Hope for Israel included further illustrations of peace
and prosperity, still viewed in an idyllic setting. Towns
and cities, destroyed by the invader, would be rebuilt and
inhabited. Vineyards and gardens, restored to ideal fertility,

would again produce the essentials of life. Land and people, separated by destruction and captivity, would know the security of peace once again. The dark clouds of doom now have passed and the dream of a new day made possible the final words, "the Lord thy God" (9:15). No longer would God be the feared avenger but the personal God of a reformed and restored people. Once again the nation could be called "my people of Israel" (9:14), and God can be referred to as "thy God." Some interpreters see in this verse the foreshadowing of the restored kingdom of David, wherein we find the germ of Isaiah's great messianic prophecies.

V. SUMMARY OF LESSONS FOR OUR DAY

The practical values to be drawn from a study of the book of Amos are transparently evident. No one has to search for hidden meanings or veiled warnings in order to apply the message to man's needs today. However, a summary of the relevant lessons may serve to fix the truths in our minds as principles for life.

1. God is the sovereign Lord of all men and all nations.

Even as Amos' message was built upon the solid foundation of God's sovereignty over the whole world, our reception of his message must begin at the same point. God does not love or judge on the basis of race, creed, or national origin. He deals with every nation and every individual on the basis of righteousness—according to the standard of God's own righteous character. He desires, even demands, that we deal with our fellowmen on the same basis of equality without discrimination.

2. The privileges of election by God involve corresponding responsibilities.

Just as Amos could never understand fully why Israel was especially chosen of God, nothing less than the grace of God can explain the privileged place which Christians have in the purposes of God. It cannot be overemphasized that privilege brings responsibility. A sense of escapism or a desire for immunity must not supplant the realization of moral opportunity and urgent obligation laid upon all who possess the gospel of Christ. Self-satisfaction and complacency can never act as substitutes for responsibility.

3. *Sin and judgment, standing as cause and effect, cannot be separated.*

The unalterable burden of Amos' message was that sin must be punished regardless of the favored status which Israel had once enjoyed. Furthermore, the impartial justice of God made necessary the pronouncement of judgment upon other nations as well. No sense of special privilege can exempt America or any other nation today from potential judgment by God. Only in the gift of God's grace to those who receive Christ can this principle be transcended, and then only through Christ's sacrifice in our stead.

4. *God demands righteousness in every area of personal and corporate life.*

Whether dealing with the individual or the nation, Amos called for a steadfast pattern of right living, refusing to accept in God's name any substitute which might be offered by men. He could never compartmentalize life into the secular and the sacred, because he viewed religion and righteousness in daily life as inseparable. While there is a special sense in which we are accounted righteous through Christ, the norm of God's righteousness as revealed in Christ must remain our ultimate goal. Jesus spoke of a somewhat similar goal when he said, "Be ye therefore perfect, even as your Father which is in heaven is perfect (Matt. 5:48). Moral judgments must always be made in the light of the revealed character of God.

5. *Worship which is unrelated to the totality of God's requirements is an insult to God.*

Amos reinterpreted the essence and function of worship in terms of God's moral demands upon his people. Whether in ancient Israel or modern America, worship by those who refuse to bring their wills and conduct into conformity with God's requirements is an insulting affront to God. Whenever ritual, form, ceremony, symbol, or method take the place of moral obedience and communion with God, true worship becomes impossible.

6. *Selfish luxury produces godless indifference to the cries of the oppressed.*

Amos saw clearly the deeper ills in Israel's society brought on by extravagant luxuries and excessive indulgence. Gross indifference to the needs of others was the evident result. Similar inordinate desires in modern society have produced a situation as deplorable as that of Amos' day. Selfish desires for personal prosperity and financial security keep many of God's spokesmen from exercising the prophetic role in denouncing injustice, immorality, corruption, and greed. How long must the less fortunate wait for successors to Amos, who embody also the compassion of Christ?

7. *Pride results in a type of self-sufficiency which crowds out the will of God.*

It was all too evident to Amos that Israel was suffering from a deep-seated pride in her own accomplishments and her favored status as chosen of God. She had lost her sense of dependence upon the one who had both chosen her and blessed her. How true this is of our self-sufficient society! An overbearing type of humanistic pride has produced a glorification of man's abilities to the point of overshadowing the glory of God. The example of Israel, as seen through the eyes of Amos, should call us back to a greater dependence upon God as creator and sustainer of all life.

8. *The true prophetic voice can never be silenced by immovable traditionalists who champion the status quo.*

Amaziah, the priest at Bethel, probably thought he had ended the effectiveness of Amos' ministry when he ordered the prophet to leave. However, since the voice of dissent was in essence the voice of God, the message has been heard repeatedly in every corner of the earth. Too often today constructive and creative criticism is branded as irresponsible, irrelevant, and heretical in nature. Surely the truths of the gospel are unchangeable. But the application of the gospel to the needs of every age requires intense self-examination, self-criticism, and adaptation by the people of God. Let us be careful in dealing with the prophetic voice in our midst lest we someday find that we have quenched the very Spirit of God.

9. *Social justice is a mandate from God, not an option to be considered by each generation.*

While Amos viewed all of life in relation to the impartial justice of a righteous God, most of his contemporaries could disassociate business from their duties at the sanctuaries. Like the leading citizens of ancient Israel, there are those today who expect God to overlook their acts of oppression and injustice as long as they perform their duties with regularity at their place of worship. For Amos and for the Christian sensitive to the rights of all men, there is no option as to the application of principles of social justice. Instead the mandate is clear: "Let justice roll down like waters, and righteousness like an everflowing stream" (5:24, RSV).

10. *The voice of God will continue to speak through the words of Amos as long as sin and injustice abound.*

Time has not blunted the incisive message of the outspoken prophet from Tekoa. His words are excitingly relevant for this age with its new and yet strikingly similar problems. After 2,700 years of application and interpretation, the cutting edge is like a two-edged sword, severing prejudices, uprooting injustice, and overturning complacency. Wherever callous indifference and sin hold sway, the Spirit of God will continue to use the book of Amos to call men back to the fundamental relations of righteous living.

FOR CLASS PREPARATION

1. Analyze ways in which men still try to escape the reality of God's presence, noting the futility of such attempts.
2. Examine the following passages from the prophetic writings which picture hope for a better day: Hosea 14:4–7; Isaiah 2:2–4; 40:3–4; 65:17–25; Zephaniah 3:11–20; Ezekiel 34:20–31; 47:7–12; Joel 3:18–21; Zechariah 14:6–11.
3. Consider seriously the lessons summarized from Amos' teaching in regard to your own relationship toward God and your fellowmen.
4. Make a list of passages from the book of Amos which speak especially to your individual needs.

For Advanced Study

1. For further discussion of the sifting process in 9:9:
   R. S. Cripps, *The Book of Amos*, pp. 265–268.
2. For added insight concerning the transformation of nature in prophetic thought:
   H. W. Robinson, *Inspiration and Revelation in the Old Testament*, pp. 28–33.
   E. C. Rust, *Nature and Man in Biblical Thought*, pp. 58–61.
3. For an examination of the problems of authorship in 9:8–15:
   S. R. Driver, *Joel and Amos* (Cambridge Bible), pp. 119–124.
   R. L. Honeycutt, *Amos and His Message*, pp. 15–17.
   G. A. Smith, *The Book of the Twelve Prophets*, I, pp. 199–205.

Suggestions for the Teacher

THE BOOK OF AMOS had a powerful message, and a somewhat unwelcomed one, for Amos' day. It has a message for our day. A deeper understanding of what God was saying—and condemning—through the prophet in his own day will help contemporary learners apply the message personally and nationally. The teacher of this book, whether pastor or layman, will be tempted to preach. After all, Amos is a book of sermons!

However, it is probable that group involvement is more likely to lead to a personal acceptance of what God is saying through the prophet. The suggestions below offer some opportunities for the use of group-learning methods. These suggestions have been made in the awareness that some classes will have only a few members, some several hundred. Many suggestions can be used in either case; others can be adapted.

Some chapters of Dr. Yates's guidebook require more study time than others. Certainly chapter 1 will require the most time. Before the study begins, divide your time and material so as to allow time appropriate to the material to be covered. The suggestions below are for your consideration:

CHAPTER 1

You probably will want to give more time to the discussion of this chapter in order to be sure class members have a good foundation for the complete study. An excellent overview of Amos, his world, and his message to the present generation would be provided by showing the film *Prophet from Tekoa*. Preview the film, make notes of questions it raises and information which can be used to supplement the film. Perhaps you will want to prepare a list of questions which you feel the film should answer. Distribute the list before the film is shown. After the film has been viewed, use the questions as guides for discussion. Fill in further information from your own background study.

If you do not use the film, Dr. Yates's guides for study will be helpful. Begin the session with a carefully thought-out word picture of Amos. Then, divide your class into three study groups. Ask each group to examine the study material under II, III, and IV of the chapter outline and to bring a report of the material from the book, along with Bible material on that subject. Ask each group to select a reporter. If the class is large, you may subdivide groups, asking each to consider the subtopics under each roman numeral of the outline.

As groups report, fill in from your own study facts needed to complete the picture of the prophet and his world.

CHAPTER 2

Begin the session by asking class members to turn to Amos 5:24 and read the verse silently. Look at the verse in another translation. Ask if the class does not feel that this is a possible statement of the theme of all of Amos' preaching. Point out the twofold nature of the theme: righteousness and justice. Lead class members to look on page 19 to find the author's statement of God's purpose through Amos.

Call on a person, already assigned, to give a report on the contributions of former prophets.

Use your own study and the study course book as resources for helping class members to understand the style and organization of the book of Amos. Ask, What literary form does Amos use with such distinction? Direct class to look in 3:4; 3:5; 3:12; 7:1-2 for examples of imagery used in Amos' messages. Guide the class through the organization of the material in Amos. (See author's discussion.) Suggest that the divisions be noted in margins of Bibles. Give a summary statement on each of the three sections.

Use suggestion 3 under "For Class Preparation" to secure discussion and personal application of "The Relevance of the Message."

CHAPTER 3

Explain the applied psychology and purposeful plan of Amos as he came to Israel with his message.

By prior assignment, have six different people prepare monologues. They will speak as if they were Israelites. They will tell one after the other what "that prophet" has said God is going to do to Damascus, Gaza, Tyre, Edom, Ammon, and Moab. (Be sure they make use of the book of Amos for information. Secure persons who will try to assume and portray these roles dramatically.) As you call on the person representing each nation, point to the location on the map.

Then explain that Amos also had a message for Judah and
Israel. Ask the people to turn to Amos 2 : 4–16 and listen for the
indictment of God's people. Now preach this part of Amos' sermon
as if the people of Judah and Israel were before you. (You may
need to write out a free translation of the passage.) Review by
asking class members to recall the *charges*—2 : 6*b*–12; and the
punishment—2 : 13–16.

Refer to suggestion 2 at the end of the chapter. Ask class to discuss any such clippings or incidents they recall.

CHAPTER 4

Arrange for a panel of good Bible students (perhaps your Adult
teachers) to prepare to discuss points I and II in the outline. Ask
half of the panel to be prepared to explore "Israel's Unique Position"; another half, "Israel's Extraordinary Responsibility." Be
ready with leading questions and statements that will guide panel
members through adequate discussion of the material.

Ask class members to look with you at Amos 3 : 9–15. Through
direct questions help them to see in these verses the special penalty
that was being predicted for Israel. Ask, What unusual thing did
Amos predict in 3 : 9–10. (Help class see that heathen nations
were being called on to judge the people of God.) Why was
destruction so inevitable for Israel? (Be sure that the basis for
the condemnation of Israel is made clear.)

To help class members make personal application of the message of Amos, guide discussion of suggestions 2 and 3 under "For
Class Preparation."

CHAPTER 5

In this chapter you can rely heavily on Scripture searching and
add your comments of interpretation. State that Amos linked
corruption in life and the validity of the worship experience. This
led him to denounce two related evils: See Amos 4 : 1–3 for lack
of concern for needy; 4 : 4–5 for superficial worship. Out of your
study show the relationship of these two evils.

Amos showed that social and religious ills would lead to destruction. He pointed out five calamities which were used to bring
judgment and repentance. Ask five different people to name these
calamities from 4 : 6,7–8,9,10, and 11. Ask the entire class to look
for Israel's response in the above verses. What phrase is repeated
in each verse?

Ask a competent member of your class to be prepared to discuss the phrase "prepare to meet thy God" and another to discuss the adequacy of God's power to bring judgment.

Lead the class to examine Jesus' reaction to superficial religious observances by a discussion of the Scripture references given in suggestion 2, "For Class Preparation."

CHAPTER 6

Divide the class into three groups. Ask each group to use the study course book and their Bibles to explore the information under I, II, or III of the outline. Allow sufficient time for study. In addition to reporting on Amos' message to Israel, each group should be prepared to answer one question concerning the assigned topic: Does this accusation or condemnation have a modern counterpart? Explain.

Call for reports from each group and encourage reaction and questions.

"The Coming Day" is a highly technical, theological matter. It will require careful explanation from the teacher. However, there is a very practical side to this section. Be sure that your explanation contains both content and application. (See John Bright's quote on page 85. Also use Scripture references under "For Class Preparation.")

CHAPTER 7

Read aloud Amos 6:1–6. Ask half of the group to follow in their Bibles, underlining phrases which are evidences of self-indulgence. Ask the remainder of the class to check words, phrases, places which seem to need explanation. List these phrases and words on the chalkboard when you have finished reading. Use the word study method to discover the meaning and message of the passage. Encourage class members to offer their own explanations. Supplement and correct as necessary.

Now ask the class to look in verse 7 to find the consequences of the sin of Israel's leaders. Find in Amos 6:8–11 the punishment to come upon the nation. Ask members to find Amos' two questions in verse 12. See if they can explain, from their study, what Amos had reference to in these questions. Turn to Proverbs 16:18 for a summary answer.

For discussion which will help class members relate the message of Amos to themselves, use suggestions 2 and 3, "For Class Preparation."

CHAPTER 8

Secure a flip chart (or prepare one from newsprint). Leave the first page blank. Then for each vision, letter on one sheet the vision and reference, and on the next sheet use a picture to visualize the plague. Use the flip chart to call attention to each vision as it is studied. Ask assigned members to read appropriate passages. (Follow the outline for chapter 8 in this book. After discussion of the first three visions, discuss Bethel's reaction, section IV, before continuing with discussion of the other vision.)

On the same flip chart, outline on one page the basic causes Amos gave for impending doom. On another page list the phrases descriptive of the day of doom. Read designated passages and discuss interpretation for Amos' day. Call for opinions as to contemporary application.

CHAPTER 9

Use the flip chart prepared for chapter 9 to review the four visions of Amos which were discussed. On another sheet have lettered the vision discussed in 9:1–4. Ask one class member to describe the vision and another to discuss the sequel to it.

In brief but clear form present the material in Amos 9:8–15. Have written on slips of paper and distributed to be read the passages from prophetic writings which picture hope for a better day.

Divide the class into small work groups. Ask each group to consider: (1) author's material under "Summary of Lessons for Our Day"; (2) suggestion 4, "For Class Preparation"; and (3) bring one recommendation of a specific action your church can take in the area of better human relations. After sufficient time for thought, call for reports from each group.

SUGGESTED AUDIO-VISUAL MATERIALS

FILMSTRIPS: *Amos and Hosea,* 35 frames; *Amos, God's Angry Man,* 46 frames; *A Plea for Justice—Amos,* 30 frames
SLIDES: "The Shepherd Amos Becomes a Preacher," "Amos the Fearless Prophet"
MOTION PICTURE: *Prophet from Tekoa,* 30 minutes

For Review and Written Work

Chapter 1

1. Describe in your own words the general appearance and personality of Amos.
2. Explain why the historical background is especially important in relation to Amos' ministry.
3. List the three most critical social problems in Israel during the days of Amos.

Chapter 2

1. Suggest and describe two ways in which Elijah's ministry set the stage for the work of Amos.
2. Outline the book of Amos around the simple fourfold divisions suggested in this book.
3. Explain why the message of Amos is still so relevant to meet the needs of our day.

Chapter 3

1. How did Amos' method of presentation involve the people in his message?
2. State briefly the sins of Israel's neighbors, and compare them with those of Israel.
3. Illustrate one or more of Amos' basic charges against Israel by means of instances within present-day America.

Chapter 4

1. In what way did Israel claim a unique place among the nations of the world? Did Amos agree?
2. Upon what basis does privilege bring responsibility?
3. Make a list of events which Amos used to illustrate his sense of prophetic insight.

Chapter 5

1. List three ways in which the leading women of Samaria were adding to the corruption of their day.

135

2. In what ways could Amos link worship and sinning? Does such a situation ever exist today?
3. How would you interpret the calamities mentioned by Amos if they were to occur today? Does God bring such warnings today?

CHAPTER 6

1. On what basis could Amos describe Israel as a dead nation?
2. Make a list of substitutes for genuine seeking of God observed by Amos. Which of these may still apply to our worship patterns?
3. How did Amos correct the superficial popular view of the Day of the Lord?

CHAPTER 7

1. Describe in your own words the "easy life" which Amos found among the leaders at Samaria, and then relate your description to the patterns of American life.
2. What was the basis of Amos' certainty concerning the coming doom upon Israel?
3. In what ways was pride the root of Israel's problems?

CHAPTER 8

1. How did the use of visions differ from the more usual forms of prophetic presentation?
2. Summarize in a brief sentence the descriptions and conclusion of each vision.
3. What charges against Amos were stated and implied by Amaziah?

CHAPTER 9

1. How did the fifth vision relate to Amos' previous remarks about Israel's worship patterns?
2. In what ways did Amos destroy the popular view that Israel would always have preferential treatment because of chosen status? (Cf. 9:7 and 3:1.)
3. Why was a dream of hope such an important part of the book of Amos?
4. What are the most relevant lessons you have learned from Amos which you plan to apply to life situations?